Anonymous

General Grant abroad

A complete account of his famous trip around the world

Anonymous

General Grant abroad
A complete account of his famous trip around the world

ISBN/EAN: 9783337146702

Printed in Europe, USA, Canada, Australia, Japan

Cover: Foto ©Andreas Hilbeck / pixelio.de

More available books at **www.hansebooks.com**

General Grant Abroad.

A COMPLETE ACCOUNT OF HIS FAMOUS

TRIP AROUND THE WORLD.

THE COUNTRIES VISITED BY GENERAL GRANT, THE ATTENTIONS SHOWN HIM, THE MEETINGS WITH DISTINGUISHED PERSONAGES, SPEECHES, COMMENTS AND CONVERSATIONS,

AND MANY

Personal Anecdotes and Incidents of Travel,

WITH

PROFUSE ILLUSTRATIONS.

"Much have I seen and known; cities of men,
And manners, climates, councils governments,
Myself not least, but honored of them all."
—TENNYSON'S ULYSSES.

CHICAGO:
BELFORDS, CLARKE & CO.
1879.

S. I. BRADBURY & SONS,
Printers, Chicago.

BLOMGREN BROS. & CO.,
Electrotypers, Chicago.

CONTENTS.

CHAPTER.	PAGE.
Biographical Sketch	IX
I.—Official Leave-Taking	23
II.—The Departure	31
III.—At Sea—Arrival at Liverpool	37
IV.—A Greeting from Old England	42
V.—Honors of London	54
VI.—On the Continent	72
VII.—Scotland, the Home of the Grants	81
VIII.—Among the English Workingmen	88
IX.—Paris	121
X.—Italy and the Mediterranean	125
XI.—Egypt and the Nile	130
XII.—Holy and Classic Lands	140
XIII.—Holland	152
VIV.—Berlin and Bismark	158
XV.—The Norse Countries	170
XVI.—Russia and Poland	177
XVII.—Austria, Bavaria and the Vineyards of France	184
XVIII.—Spain and Portugal	188
XIX.—General Grant and the Irish	195
XX.—In India	203
XXI.—In Siam	216
XXII.—China and the Celestials	231
XXIII.—Japan	249
XXIV.—The Pacific Voyage	273
XXV.—Home Again	283

BIOGRAPHICAL SKETCH.

The reader is about to accompany the most illustrious man of this age in a Trip Around the World. Before entering upon the journey, it may be well to refresh one's recollection of the more salient points in his life. This prefatory biographical sketch will aim to present such facts in the record of Gen. Grant as will add interest to the narrative which is to follow, as well as to explain the phenomenal reception which awaited him wherever he went, and made his tour the most remarkable one in all history.

Gen. Grant is of Scotch descent, coming from a family which had for its motto these words, peculiarly prophetic of the man who was to render the name deathless: "Stand fast, stand firm, stand true." The earliest American traces of the family are found in Connecticut. Captain Noah Grant, the General's great-grandfather, and also a great-grand uncle, were soldiers in the old French war. Noah Grant, Jr., was a lieutenant in the battle of Lexington, and after the Revolutionary war he settled in Westmoreland county, Pennsylvania, where Jesse R. Grant, father of our hero was born and where he learned the tanners trade. He removed to Point Pleasant, Clermont county, Ohio, where the General, the eldest of six children, was born, April 27, 1822. The father was a good business man, upright and sagacious, enjoying rather more than the ordinary degree of prosperity. He lived to see his son President of the United States, dying at Covington, Kentucky, in the year 1874. The General's mother is still alive, and in remarkable possession of her mental faculties. She resides with her daughter, Mrs. Corbin, in New Jersey. She is a devout Methodist in her religious convictions. It is from her, it is said, that her distinguished son inherits his more marked characteristics.

Gen. Grant was christened Hiram Ulysses. He owes his change of name to Ulysses Simpson, to the blunder of the Congressman who procured his appointment as a West Point Cadet, a mistake he tried, but in vain, to have rectified. The War Department having enrolled him as Ulysses S. Grant, would not be at the trouble to change it. Simpson was his mother's maiden name. He was known at West Point as "Uncle Sam." Although only seventeen years old when he entered that Military Academy, his gravity of character, hardly less than his initials, U. S., justified the appellation.

At West Point his career was unmarked by any noteworthy feature. The same remark holds true of his army record immediately succeeding his graduation. It covered a period of eleven years, during which time he served honorably in the Mexican war as a Lieutenant, taking part in every battle, except that of Buena Vista, and receiving three brevets for gallantry. He remained in the service until 1854. During that time he saw much of the evil workings of our pernicious Indian system, acquiring knowledge whic enabled him to deal intelligently with the Indian problem, as the executive head of the nation.

When Captain Grant resigned his commission in the army, he became a farmer in Gravois, Missouri, twenty miles from St. Louis. He remained there about six years, and then joined his brothers in the leather business at Galena. Those seven years of private life were uneventful. He may almost be said to have hibernated, awaiting the time when a great emergency would demand his great services.

When the South raised the standard of revolt, Captain Grant was among the first to offer himself to whatever duty might be assigned him. At first he assisted the Adjutant-General of Illinois in the clerical work of his office. His military education enabled him to be quite useful, but he had no taste for that sort of thing. His fellow-townsman, Hon. E. B. Washburne, then a leading member of Congress, seemed to have had from the first some appreciation of his capacity, and determined that the modest Captain should have a fair chance; a determination which was of incalculable benefit to the country on more than one occasion during the earlier years of the war. Agreeably to his recommendation, Gov. Yates made Capt. Grant Col. Grant, assigning him to the command of the 21st regiment of Illinois Infantry. He joined his regiment at once, and soon brought it into a good state of discipline.

On the seventh of August President Lincoln commissioned Col. Grant as a Brigadier-General of volunteers, the commission dating back to May 17. It was then that the General's real life began. At the age of thirty-nine he entered upon his career of usefulness and glory. His first important service was the seizure of Paducah, at the mouth of the Tennessee river. His first battle was Belmont, fought Nov. 7, 1861.

From that time on, until he became the acknowledged hero of the war, he was one of its central figures. Space does not permit a narration of the gradual steps by which he rose in command, and of the various battles which he fought between Belmont and Appomattox. The fall of Fort Donelson was his first great victory, and it sent a thrill of exultant hope throughout the country. From that time dates his national fame. There were not wanting those who thus early saw in him the great conqueror of peace. An Illinois Colonel, since famous as the greatest orator and debator, wrote in a private letter, "This war will not close till Grant closes it."

The fall of Vicksburg put an end to all serious and really injurious cavil about his proper rank as a soldier. Malice, envy and slander were henceforth powerless to dim the luster of his glory, and make the path of his promotion a roadbed of thorns. Donelson fell in February, 1862; Shiloh was fought in April following; a few months after, operations against Vicksburg were suggested by Grant, and in the same year commenced culminating in a surrender, which made his name second only to Lincoln in the loyal hearts of the country. It was then that the people were first made acquainted with the electric felicity of his epigrammatic style. To the enemy's overtures for capitulation he replied: "No terms other than unconditional and immediate surrender can be accepted. I propose to move immediately upon your works." That was the end of the siege. July 4, 1863, Vicksburg fell, and everywhere Gen. Grant was recognized as the foremost soldier of the war.

Early in 1864 the General was made the military head of the entire army, then numbering about 700,000 men. He was the first and of course the only General put in command of all the forces. The rank of Lieutenant-General, which had lapsed with the death of Gen. Scott, was revived for that express purpose by act of Congress. (It was not until July 25, 1866, that the rank of General was created for him.) It was in March that Major-General Grant became Lieutenant-General, and assumed complete control of military operations. He "made haste slowly" to justify the confidence reposed in him.

Gen. Sherman's capture of Atlanta in the summer following, and his subsequent march to the sea, narrowed the war down to a question of the fall of Richmond and the surrender of Lee's army of the Potomac. Gradually the closing-in process, or "rounding-up," as herders say, was pursued, and April 9, 1865, saw the death-gasp of the Confederacy. There was a great deal of hard fighting in Virginia before the final blow was struck, and some have criticized it as an unnecessary waste of life; but it involved far less loss of life than a summer campaign would have done, and must in all fairness be conceded to have been the best ending of the war which was possible under the exigencies then existing.

From the spring of 1865 to the spring of 1869 Gen. Grant enjoyed comparative rest. He was the head of the army in a time of profound peace. With the political turmoil of the ever memorable and very stormy administration of Andrew Johnson, he did not interfere. He was at Washington, and the "rising sun" in the Presidential horizon; but he succeeded in keeping aloof from responsibilities foreign to his official duties. Even although his name was continually dragged before the public in connection with politics. From August 12, 1867, to January 14, 1868, he was Secretary of War *ad interim*, assigned to that duty by his superior officer, Andrew Johnson, *ex-officio* Commander-in-Chief of the Army and Navy. It is also true that the President attempted to make him a party to his unseemly conflict with the Senate of the United States over the re-instatement as Secretary of War, of Hon. Edwin M. Stanton. But the General's calm fidelity to the strict line of duty saved him from any real entanglement of the kind. It early became a foregone conclusion, however, that the

Republican party would nominate him for President in 1868, and when the Republican National Convention of that year met at Chicago, in May, there was no name mentioned for the head of the ticket but his. He was nominated by acclamation, amid the wildest enthusiasm.

It may be remarked here that all through the public career of Gen. Grant, he has been peculiar in this: that while he has often been the subject of bitter jealousy and mean animosity, every honor bestowed upon him has come at last, without serious opposition. The promotions he won in war were so clearly deserved, and their bestowal was so necessary to the public, that before the goal was really reached all opposition faded away. No war hero at all comparable to him ever disputed his right to the front rank. Generals Sherman, Sheridan and Thomas freely and fairly accorded him the place assigned him. Twice he has been nominated for the Presidency by the Republican party, and on neither occasion was there a competitor. The third time he was talked of, but he stubbornly refused the use of his name. He never knew what it was to scheme and maneuver for the promotion of personal ambition, and this is the very key to his greatness and popularity. Whatever he has had to do he has done with single reference to its accomplishment. He has a genius for concentration on the present which is most rare and useful. He has never once crossed the bridge until he reached the stream, or, rather, never used pontoons until he needed them.

With the political campaign which culminated in his election to the presidency in 1868 he had nothing to do. He made no attempt to influence the voters of the country. He stood upon his record as a soldier and his cordial endorsement of the platform of his party, which platform was simply a pledge to secure by appropriate legislation the fruits of the war, and to deal honestly in matters of finance. To those cardinal principles he gave his entire assent. His opponent was the most popular Democrat in the country, Horatio Seymour. The result of the election was that Grant carried all but six States, receiving 214 electoral votes, to 80 cast for Seymour.

On the fourth of March, 1869, General Grant became President Grant. It would be quite foreign to this sketch to follow in any detail those eight years from his first inauguration to his official leave-taking, the fifth of March, 1877. It will be enough to point out the cardinal features of his great civil service.

During the last ten years the subject of civil service reform has engrossed public attention to quite an extent. The term has become very trite; but not so trite as the reform is important. President Grant did not begin its

B

agitation or espouse the cause in the spirit of a *doctrinaire*. It is none the less, or, rather, all the more true, that he began his Administration by inaugurating the reformation needed. The real evil was the usurpation by Congress of the executive function in making executive appointments.

The successor in the presidency of John Quincy Adams had for his motto the demoralizing doctrine, "To the victor belong the spoils." From Andrew Jackson to Andrew Johnson, covering a period of about forty years, the idea that appointive Federal offices are party patronage, or spoils, obtained; and as a consequence the representatives in Congress of the party in power came to regard the dispensing of patronage in their respective districts as among their perquisites. Custom assigned certain general appointments to the Senate, and the more local offices to the House. As an inevitable result every office-holder was the vassal of some Congressman, his tenure of office depending upon his fealty to "the lord of the feif." As a matter of course this subversion, in effect, of the constitutional distribution of authority between the executive and the legislative branches of the Government became a very serious evil. Its reform has at last been carried so far as to have wrought a very marked and wholesome change.

President Grant began the reformation by frequent, although not universal, disregard of the precedent in question. He freely exercised his personal judgment in these matters, when his knowledge of applicants rendered that feasible. He drove the plowshare of reformation through the turf and weeds of established abuse, heedless of the frantic outcries of professional politicians. He so far succeeded in uprooting the evil, that his successor was elected on a platform distinctly and strongly pledging him to the maintenance of the policy inaugurated.

There were those, however, who desired to carry the change much further, and make civil service reform mean: "Once in office, always in office." It was attempted by some to fasten upon the Federal Government an un-republican and dangerous species of barnacleism. With that theory of civil service, President Grant had no sympathy. He thus confronted antipodal opposition. That opposition culminated in the "Liberal" movement which resulted in the phenomenal presidential candidature of that greatest and best of journalists, Horace Greeley, in 1872, from whose defeat may be said to date the establishment of a common-sense sort of civil service reform.

We have first spoken of this feature of the Grant Administration, because it first came to the surface, albeit its accomplishment was so long delayed, and the honor of it is shared by the present Administration.

The work of reconstructing the South had been mainly effected during the Johnson Administration, so far as concerned congressional legislation and constitutional amendments, the President's veto power being impotent to arrest progress. With the inauguration of U. S. Grant, the executive department of the government became entirely harmonious with that policy of reconstruction, which was, universal amnesty and universal suffrage. With the utmost fidelity Gen. Grant sought to eradicate from the rebel element the animosities of the war, and secure the colored people in the enjoyment of their political rights. In neither was he successful to an extent at all satisfactory. By the enforcement of the law designed to break up the Ku-Klux-Klan, a secret organization, having for its object the intimidation of negro citizens, he checked for a time the outlawries of the South; but when the clamor against "bayonet rule" secured the repeal of that law, he was without the authority adequate to the restraint of what came to be known as "bull-dozing." In the light of what the Administration accomplished before the repeal referred to, it is evident that Gen. Grant has the genius for maintaining the political rights guaranteed to the citizen by national law, under adequate legislation; but his steadfast refusal to interfere, when importuned in the last days of his Administration, show that he had too much respect for the law to usurp authority not duly vested in him.

In accordance with the policy to which he was pledged in advance of his election, Gen. Grant steadily and greatly reduced the national debt. He also firmly resisted all attempts at inflation. Under his Administration the plan of resumption of specie payment was adopted, which has since been carried to such a glorious consummation. He was the staunch enemy of all wild schemes of finance, and the successful promoter of an "honest money" policy.

The feature of his Administration which is likely to be widest and longest remembered, was the successful attempt to apply the principle of arbitration to international difficulties.

Among the unsettled war issues which came down to him from the succeeding Administration, was the "Alabama question." The amount of bad feeling between the United States and Great Britain, over the depredations of that piratical craft and kindred privateers of the war, was alarming. Both countries seemed ripe for a conflict of arms. In vain had that great peacemaker, Secretary Seward, tried to settle the matter. The problem was entirely unsolved when it was passed over to President Grant and Secretary Fish; but before the first term of the Grant Administration had expired, every vestige of the war cloud had disappeared, and before the whole world had been set an example of peaceable adjustment in international controversies which of itself ought to render the names of Grant and Gladstone immortal.

Of the domestic life of Gen. Grant little need be said beyond the well known fact that it is irreproachable and exceedingly fortunate. He was married in 1848 to Julia Dent, the daughter of a leading merchant in St. Louis. The more than queenly grace with which Mrs. Grant has borne herself in all the circumstances of her life are a glory to womanhood. Four children complete the family circle, Col. F. D. Grant, of Gen. Sheridan's staff; Mrs. Nellie Sartoris, whose home is in England, and two sons who are still quite young men, U. S. Grant, Jr., and Jesse R. Grant. It is enough to say that the children are all, in their modest and sensible way, worthy their illustrious parentage.

It need only be added that Gen. Grant is now, at the age of fifty-seven, in the prime of robust manhood, with the prospect of a future that can hardly add to his glory, but may swell the volume of his usefulness.

CHAPTER I.

OFFICIAL LEAVE-TAKING.

Close of General Grant's Presidential Term— The Political Excitement of the Time— The Inuguration of President Hayes — The Decalogue Above the Constitution — General Grant Out of the Harness — Last Days at Washington — Enjoying his Freedom — Feeling of the People toward him.

The winter of 1876–77 was peculiarly tempestuous, politically speaking. The campaign which it was expected would close with the election in November, seemed then only just begun. When once the smoke of the battle had cleared off, and the several States had sent in their returns, it was found that the result was so very close that each of the great parties stoutly, and no doubt honestly, claimed the victory. The excitement was intense, and everybody seemed fairly wild with resolve to secure the fruits of victory.

In the midst of all this frenzy and peril, President Grant was perfectly cool. He had taken no part in the campaign, except that it was well known that his sympathies were with the Republican party. He had shown no anxiety beyond a desire to have a free and fair election, and a determination to do his official duty in the preservation of the peace. During that memorable winter he took very little part in the proceedings; none, in fact, beyond making it perfectly plain to both parties and the whole country that when his term of office expired he should surrender the reins of government, then in his hands, to the lawfully elected successor. That was all there was to it, so far as he was concerned. But that was a great deal. Had he been in the least disposed to execute a *coup d' etat*, or to allow one in his interest, the circumstances were peculiarly favorable therefor. No ruler ever prolonged his term of power, or changed from a representative and elective head to a sovereign, with as good excuse for so doing as President Grant had, or might easily have created. But there never was a moment when any American citizen had the slightest thought that he contemplated anything of the kind.

Previous to the campaign a good deal had been said, in one way or another, about "Cæsarism," and attempts were made in some quarters to carry the impression that Gen. Grant was "the man on horseback," and all that sort of thing. He had under him a force of civilians in the discharge of executive duties amounting, all told, to nearly one hundred thousand, very many of them influential politicians. The charge was that with their help he would perpetuate his administration beyond the second term to which he had been elected. Not only did his name not appear in the National Republican Convention at Cincinnati in the spring of 1876, but when extraordinary facility for usurpation presented itself in the succeeding winter he was so far above temptation as to be entirely free from suspicion of Cæsarism. It may well be said of him, "Nothing in his [official] life became him so as the leaving of it." In the permanent history of the United States, that final feature of his administration will be the most prominent feature of both terms, and he will be honored, wherever Republican principles are maintained, as the American President who converted the especial opportunity for Imperialism into the strongest possible assurance that this Republic has nothing to fear from that rock, albeit so many self-governments have foundered upon it.

The fourth of March, 1877, came upon Sunday. The Constitution of the United States by providing that the inauguration of a new President should occur upon that day of that month, evidently designed to ignore the day of the week entirely. But following a precedent and deferring to the religious sentiment of the country, it was tacitly agreed that Gen. Grant should vacate his office in favor of President Hayes, on Monday, March 5th. In the Electoral Commission work he had had no part, except to sign the bill passed by both parties creating that Board of Arbitration. He did not come in for any part of the execrations called out by that Commission. Those who were the most vehement in denouncing the new President's official title as fraudulent, conceded the propriety of Gen. Grant's course in the matter. Had Mr. Tilden taken the oath of office, and appeared thus as a competitor, it might have been different. As it was, Gen. Grant became a private citizen without having the least responsibility for the settlement of the contest for the succession. Herein he was fortunate, his good fortune being the result of his uniform and perfect adherence to the policy of minding one's own business. He neither evaded nor assumed anything.

Notwithstanding the religious scruples which prevented the inauguration being on Sunday, that was a busy day at the National Capital, and the last day of President Grant's official life was occupied in passing upon bills sent him by Congress. A very large amount of legislation was completed March 4th, 1877. The next day was wholly given to the ceremonies appropriate to the transition. At a little after ten o'clock in the morning, the President elect, accompanied by his friend and future chief cabinet officer, John Sherman, called at the White House and was cordially greeted by the retiring President. A few mutual friends were present, and a brief chat, without the slightest formality and restraint, followed. The ceremonies of inauguration were in the Senate Chamber, where the retiring President was simply a spectator.

At the conclusion, the new President and the ex-President returned together to the Executive Mansion, and the latter disappeared from public view. The next day a Washington correspondent wrote: "President Grant went walking to-day with a cane in his hand and a cigar in his mouth, and looked about him as if it was a new world in which he found himself." And such indeed it was. For half a generation he had been continually in public life. From the evening of the day when news reached his home in Galena that Sumter had been fired on, his whole thoughts had been upon his country. On that evening a "war meeting" was held there, as in many other places; and Congressman Washburne, in calling the meeting to order, proposed as chairman, "our old Mexican soldier, Capt. Grant." In war and in peace he had served the country in a military capacity eight years, followed by eight years of chief magistracy. To be free from all public cares must have been an inexpressible relief. He spent several days in strolling and riding about the Capital, enjoying his vacation. He remained there about three weeks, taking no part in the heated discussions and competitions incident to the new President and his Southern policy. Keenly appreciating the embarrassments of the situation, and knowing the danger of misconstruing his casual remarks, he refrained from anything that might tend to annoy President Hayes.

A dispatch from the Capital dated March 26th, says: "Ex-President Grant left Washington last night for Cincinnati, where he will remain four or five days, going thence to Chicago and Galena. Going East he will stop at Harrisburg to enjoy trout fishing in the vicinity, and then proceed to Philadelphia, at which port, about the 10th of May, he will take passage for Europe, with members of his family. Since his term of office expired many persons sought his influence in their behalf, with the new Administration, but they did not secure it." That remained true to the end.

From this time on, until his arrival at Philadelphia, according to the foregoing programme, Gen. Grant was allowed to come and go as unheeded as the most retiring gentleman could desire. He seemed to be dismissed from the popular mind. He was neither censured nor praised. Other objects engaged the attention of the public. He was no novelty, nor was he a power in the land. Abstaining from any participation in public affairs, he was let alone most effectually. None tried to win his good opinion in view of any future contingency. On the contrary, it seemed to be universally taken for granted that U. S. Grant had closed his public career for sure, and would be as completely buried as any other ex-President the country had had. There was, apparently, an entire suspension of feeling toward him, of any kind whatever; and when, a little later, he embarked for a foreign land, the demonstration in his honor at the port of departure excited no emotion in the country at large. How long this apathy would have continued had he retired to his home, it is impossible to surmise; but that it existed without break until after his departure is certain. In a word, Gen. Grant's official leave-taking was his retirement from public gaze and thought, until extraordinary honors began to be showered upon him abroad, since which time his own countrymen have been quite generally and thoroughly alive to his existence and prominence, he being universally recognized as the most distinguished American of his age.

CHAPTER II.

THE DEPARTURE.

A Flying Trip West—The Return to Philadelphia—Final Preparations—The Breakfast at Mr. Childs'—Farewell Greetings—Message from President Hayes—General Sherman's Speech—General Grant's Response—Down the Delaware.—On Board the "Indiana"—Off for Europe.

After the formal and official leave-taking at Washington were over, Gen. Grant made a brief visit to his old home in the West, and then returned to Philadelphia to complete final arrangements for his departure for Europe, and to spend a week with his old and intimate friend, Geo. W. Childs, Esq. The day following his arrival in Philadelphia (May 10th,) the opening of the "Permanent Exhibition" Building took place; and

Gen. Grant attended the opening exercises. The ensuing three days were spent in enjoying the hospitalities of prominent citizens of Philadelphia, and on the 14th he attended a reception given in his honor by the Union League Club. On the 16th a procession of soldiers' orphans marched by Mr. Childs' residence, Gen. Grant and Gen. Sherman standing on the steps of the house and greeting the little ones pleasantly as they passed. Twelve hundred veteran soldiers and sailors afterwards paid their respects to Gen. Grant in Independence Hall. In the evening he was serenanded at Mr. Childs' residence, the house being brilliantly illuminated and a vast crowd being present.

On the morning of Gen. Grant's departure from Philadelphia, a distinguished company were entertained by Mr. Childs, at a breakfast given in the General's honor; among the guests being Gen. Sherman, Governor Hartranft, and Hon. Hamilton Fish. After breakfast Gen. Grant and a party of friends went on board the steamer "Magenta" and proceeded down the river to where the steamship "Indiana" was waiting to begin her ocean voyage—Mrs. Grant and her friends being conveyed by the United States revenue cutter "Hamilton." As the two vessels passed down the Delaware, they were enthusiastically cheered by the crowds of people who lined the wharves, while all the river craft was gaily decorated with flags and bunting.

At Girard Point a short stoppage was made, and a telegram from the President of the United States was received by Gen. Grant, as follows:

"NEW YORK, May 17th, 1877.
"GENERAL GRANT, *Philadelphia:*

"Mrs. Hayes joins me in heartiest wishes that you and Mrs. Grant may have a prosperous voyage, and, after a happy visit abroad, a safe return to your friends and country.

"R. B. HAYES."

To this the following response was sent by Gen. Grant:

"STEAMER 'MAGENTA,'
"DELAWARE RIVER, MAY 17th, 11 O'CLOCK A. M.
"PRESIDENT HAYES, *Executive Mansion, Washington:*

"DEAR SIR:—Mrs. Grant joins me in thanks to you and Mrs. Hayes for your kind wishes, and your message received on board this boat just as we are pushing out from the wharf. We unite in returning our cordial greetings, and in expressing our best wishes for your health, happiness and success in your most responsible position. Hoping to return to my country to find it prosperous in business, and with cordial feelings renewed between all sections,

"I am, dear sir, truly yours,
"U. S. GRANT."

Before the party left the "Magenta," luncheon was served, at which a few parting toasts were offered and responses made. After proposing as the first toast of the occasion, "God-speed to our honored guest, Ulysses S. Grant," Mayor Stokeley, of Philadelphia, spoke briefly as follows:

"GENERAL GRANT: As I now feel that it is necessary to draw these festivities to a close, I must speak for the City of Philadelphia. I am sure that I express the feelings of

Philadelphia as I extend to you my hand, that I give to you the hands and the hearts of Philadelphia" (cheers), "and as we part with you now, it is the hope of Philadelphia that God will bless you with a safe voyage and a happy return; and with these few words I say God bless you, and God direct and care for you in your voyage across the ocean."

General Grant's reply was full of feeling, and he was visibly affected as he said:

"MR. MAYOR AND GENTLEMEN: I feel much overcome with what I have heard. When the first toast was offered I supposed the last words here for me had been spoken, and I feel overcome by the sentiments to which I have listened, and which I feel I am altogether inadequate to respond to. I don't think that the compliments ought all be paid to me or any one man in either of the positions which I was called upon to fill.

"That which I accomplished—which I was able to accomplish—I owe to the assistance of able lieutenants. I was so fortunate as to be called to the first position in the army of the nation, and I had the good fortune to select lieutenants who could have filled" (turning to Sherman)—"had it become necessary I believe some of these lieutenants could have filled my place may be better than I did." (Cries of "No.") "I do not, therefore, regard myself as entitled to all the praise.

"I believe that my friend Sherman could have taken my place as a soldier as well as I could, and the same will apply to Sheridan." (Cheers.) "And I believe, finally, that if our country ever comes into trial again, young men will spring up equal to the occasion, and if one fails, there will be another to take his place." (Great cheers.) "Just as there was if I had failed. I thank you again and again, gentlemen, for the hearty and generous reception I have had in your great city." (Prolonged cheers.)

In response to a toast to his own health, Gen. Sherman used these well-chosen words:

"MR. MAYOR AND GENTLEMEN: This proud welcome along the shores of the Delaware demands a response. Gen. Grant leaves here to-day with the highest rewards of his fellow-citizens, and on his arrival on the other side there is no doubt he will be welcomed by his friends with as willing hands and warm hearts as those he leaves behind. Ex-President Grant—Gen. Grant—while you, his fellow-citizens, speak of him as Ex-President Grant, I cannot but think of the times of war, of Gen. Grant, President of the United States for eight years, yet I cannot but think of him as Gen. Grant of Fort Donelson. I think of him as the man who, when the country was in the hour of peril, restored its hopes when he marched triumphant into Fort Donelson. After that none of us felt the least doubt as to the future of our country, and therefore, if the name of Washington is allied with the birth of our country, that of Grant is forever identified with its preservation, its perpetuation. It is not here alone on the shores of the Delaware, that the people love and respect you, but in Chicago and St. Paul, and in the far-off San Francisco, the prayers go up to-day that your voyage may be prosperous and pleasant, and that you may have a safe and happy return. General Grant" (extending his hand), "God bless you, God bless you, and grant you a pleasant journey and a safe return to your native land."

Brief complimentary speeches were also made by Governor Hartranft, Ex-Secretaries Fish and Chandler, and other guests.

The steamship "Indiana" was reached at a little before three o'clock, and Gen. and Mrs. Grant and their son Jesse passed on board. The last words of parting were now said; and amid the waving of handkerchiefs and hearty cheers from the crowded steamer, a salute of twenty-one guns from the cutter "Hamilton" and shrill whistles from the rest of the fleet, the "Indiana," with her distinguished freight, steamed slowly out to sea.

CHAPTER III.

AT SEA—ARRIVAL AT LIVERPOOL.

General Grant as a Sailor—His Enjoyment of the Voyage—Companionable Qualities—The Captain's Opinion of Grant as a Talker—"No Politicians Need Apply"—Off the British Coast—Queenstown—Arrival at Liverpool.

The steamer which bore General Grant across the Atlantic, on the first voyage of his memorable trip around the world, the "Indiana," was a magnificent vessel plying between Philadelphia and Liverpool, and belonging to the only American line of steamships crossing the Atlantic Ocean. With the characteristic habit of preferring the institutions of his own country, it was General Grant's wish to cross the sea in an

American vessel. The "Indiana" left Newcastle, on the Delaware river, thirty-five miles below Philadelphia, on the afternoon of the 17th day of May, and arrived at Liverpool on the 28th, making the passage in eleven days. The weather was generally rough, and most of the passengers, including Mrs. Grant, suffered more or less from seasickness; but the General did not miss a meal. The voyage was for him a thoroughly enjoyable and happy one, and was an auspicious beginning of the remarkable series of travels which were to occupy two and a half years of time, and extend around the globe, unmarred by a single accident.

On this outward voyage, General Grant was thoroughly at his ease, and developed sociable and companionable qualities which no one, excepting possibly a few intimate friends, had before suspected. He gave himself up thoroughly to comfort, and to the enjoyment of the scenes and experiences through which he was passing for the first time, as well as to the new and grateful sense of relief from the heavy cares and burdens which he had carried so long. Like most hard workers, the General knows how to rest. After sixteen years' continuous and arduous service for his country, he doubtless felt that he had well earned a vacation, and meant to enjoy it to the utmost. When, from the deck of the "Indiana," he watched the shores of his native land recede and fade from sight, he left with them the burdens and responsibilities of public life. He remarked that he "felt better than for sixteen years," from the fact that he had no letters to read and no telegraphic dispatches to attend to. It was this philosophic feeling of contentment and satisfaction, together with his unvarying good health and cheerfulness, that enabled him to enjoy this ocean trip so thoroughly, and to contribute materially to the pleasure of his fellow-passengers.

The voyage was, indeed, a new revelation of the character of General Grant. The retiring and taciturn, almost brusque, manner which had distinguished him during his public career, was dropped as if it had been a mask which had covered his true character, and he became one of the most genial and companionable of men. He showed himself a ready and entertaining talker, and surprised all by the extent of his information, the force and aptness of his comments, and the unsuspected grace and charm of his conversation. Captain Sargent, the commanding officer of the ship, described him as one of the most interesting and agreeable talkers he had ever met—and he has met a great many. "There is no one," said Captain Sargent, "who can make himself more entertaining or agreeable in his conversation, than General Grant, *when nobody has an axe to grind.*" When the General was in office, he learned to suspect nearly every one who approached him with having some "axe to grind;" and hence his habit of reserve and silence during his public career, and behind which he shielded himself from importunate or injudicious friends.

There was one subject, however, upon which the characteristic caution of General Grant showed itself. He would not converse upon American topics; and this course he rigidly adhered to throughout his entire trip. The good sense and propriety of this policy were so well recognized, that but few attempts were made to draw the General into political conversations; and these were speedily abandoned. Upon all other subjects he was a ready talker as well as an appreciative listener; and by his cordial and genial manners he readily won the friendship and admiration of his fellow-passengers, even of those among them who had opposed him most bitterly in politics. In smoking and chatting upon deck or in the smoking cabin, in reading or playing games, in watching the varying phases of sea and sky, and enjoying the many novel experiences of an ocean trip, the time passed rapidly and pleasantly away.

On the tenth day the passengers on the "Indiana" got a glimpse of Fastnet Light through the fog off the Irish coast. Here the vessel was detained eight hours by the fog, and at 7 o'clock in the evening (May 27th), entered Queenstown harbor. A tug soon came alongside, bringing a number of prominent citizens to welcome General Grant to Ireland. The General received the delegation in the cabin of the "Indiana," and listened with much satisfaction to their kindly expressions of friendship and welcome, to which he responded briefly and gracefully, promising to accept their proffered hospitality at a later period of his journey. The tug brought many letters and despatches to him, among them invitations to dinners and receptions, from the leading public men of England. Leaving Queenstown, the "Indiana" again put out to sea; and the next afternoon (May 28th) she arrived at Liverpool, where a bright and exhilerating day, with vast crowds of people, and a great display of flags in the town and upon the shipping along the Mersey river, waited to extend a greeting and a welcome to the distinguished visitor.

CHAPTER IV.

A GREETING FROM OLD ENGLAND.

A Graceful Act by the State Department—General Grant and our Representatives Abroad—The Reception at Liverpool—Address of the Mayor—Seeing the City—Banquet at the Mayor's Home—The General's Little Speech—Arrival at Manchester—Address of Welcome—General Grant as a Speech-Maker—A Surprise to his Friends—His Remarks at Manchester, Salford, Leicester and Bedford—First Impressions of England—Letter to a Friend in this Country.

About the time of General Grant's departure from Philadelphia, the State Department at Washington issued to its representatives abroad the following official circular regarding his foreign travels:

"DEPARTMENT OF STATE,
WASHINGTON, May 23d, 1877.

"*To the Diplomatic and Consular Officers of the United States.*

"GENTLEMEN: General Ulysses S. Grant, the late President of the United States, sailed from Philadelphia on the 17th inst., for Liverpool.

"The route and extent of his travels, as well as the duration of his sojourn abroad, were alike undetermined at the time of his departure, the object of his journey being to secure a few months of rest and recreation after sixteen years of unremitting and devoted labor in the military and civil service of his country.

"The enthusiastic manifestations of popular regard and esteem for General Grant shown by the people in all parts of the country that he has visited since his retirement from official life, and attending his every appearance in public from the day of that retirement up to the moment of his departure for Europe, indicate beyond question the high place he holds in the grateful affections of his countrymen.

"Sharing in the largest measure this general public sentiment, and at the same time expressing the wishes of the President, I desire to invite the aid of the Diplomatic and Consular Officers of the Government to make his journey a pleasant one should he visit their posts. I feel already assured that you will find patriotic pleasure in anticipating the wishes of the Department by showing him that attention which is due from every officer of the Government to a citizen of the Republic so signally distinguished both in official service and personal renown.

"I am, Gentlemen,
"Your obedient servant,
"WM. M. EVARTS."

This was a graceful and appropriate attention from the State Department. While General Grant went abroad simply as a private citizen of the United States, yet the fame of his grand achievements had preceded him throughout the civilized world, and his merits and renown were sure to meet with special recognition in the countries which he was to visit. It was fitting, therefore, that he should go abroad not only with the hearty and enthusiastic good-wishes of his countrymen, but with a distinct expression of their esteem and gratitude, in credentials from the government in which he had held such distinguished stations.

The foreign official agents of the United States responded cordially to the sentiments of Mr. Evarts' note, and did all in their power to add to the pleasure of General Grant's visit to their respective countries. The first to pay his respects to the General, upon his landing on English soil, was our Consul at London, General Adam Badeau, on old-time friend and aide-de-camp of General Grant. The Mayor of Liverpool and many prominent citizens were also at the dock to welcome General Grant, whom the Mayor addressed formally as follows:

"GENERAL GRANT: I am proud that it has fallen to my lot, as Chief Magistrate of Liverpool, to welcome to the shores of England so distinguished a citizen of the United

States. You have, sir, stamped your name on the history of the world by your brilliant career as a soldier, and still more as a statesman in the interests of peace. In the name of Liverpool, whose interests are so closely allied with your great country, I bid you heartily welcome, and I hope Mrs. Grant and yourself will enjoy your visit to Old England."

General Grant responded in a brief expression of thanks for his reception, and for the good wishes of his English friends; after which the party were taken in carriages to the Adelphi Hotel. In the evening they were entertained by the Mayor, at his splendid country residence, where they spent the night.

The following day was spent in visiting the prominent sights of Liverpool, under the escort of the Mayor and other citizens. They took a short ride on the river upon a small steamer, General Grant being specially interested in the commercial activity of which the city bore such abundant evidence, and in the extensive dock improvements along the river wall. After visiting the Town Hall and the celebrated Liverpool Free Library, a grand banquet was given by the Mayor at his city residence in honor of his distinguished guests. At this banquet two hundred and fifty persons were present, including the leading officials and prominent citizens of the place. General Grant's speech at the banquet was a pleasant, off-hand affair, and was received with the greatest enthusiasm. In response to a complimentary toast from the Mayor, the General said:

"MR. MAYOR AND GENTLEMEN: You have alluded to the hearty reception given to me on my first landing on the soil of Great Britain, and the expectations of the Mayor that this reception would be equaled throughout the island have been more than realized. It has been far beyond anything I could have expected. (Cheers.) I am a soldier, and the gentlemen here beside me know that a soldier must die. I have been a President, but we know that the term of the presidency expires, and when it has expired he is no more than a dead soldier. (Laughter and cheers.) But, gentlemen, I have met with a reception that would have done honor to any living person. (Cheers.) I feel, however, that the compliment has been paid, not to me, but to my country. I cannot help but at this moment being highly pleased at the good feeling and good sentiment which now exist between the two peoples who of all others should be good friends. We are of one kindred, of one blood, of one language, and of one civilization, though in some respects we believe that we, being younger, surpass the mother country. (Laughter.) You have made improvements on the soil and the surface of the earth which we have not yet done, which we do not believe will take us as long as it took you. (Laughter and applause.) I heard some military remarks which impressed me a little at the time—I am not quite sure whether they were in favor of the volunteers or against them. I can only say from my own observation that you have as many troops at Aldershott as we have in the whole of our regular army, notwithstanding we have many thousands of miles of frontier to guard and hostile Indians to control. But if it became necessary to raise a volunteer force, I do not think we could do better than to follow your example. General Fairchild [the American Consul at Liverpool] and myself are examples of volunteers who came forward when their assistance was necessary, and I have no doubt that if you ever needed such services you would have support from your reserve forces and volunteers, far more effective than you can conceive." (Cheers.)

At Manchester, whither General Grant proceeded on the following day (May 30th), substantially the same experience was had as at Liverpool. A deputation of the City Council met the General at the station and escorted him to the Town Hall, where he was formally received by the Mayor as the guest of the city. After visiting some of the immense establishments which have given Manchester its reputation as a manufacturing town, the party were conducted to the Royal Exchange, where a large assemblage, including the members of Parliament from Manchester and many of the leading merchants and officials of the town, received them. An address of welcome to General Grant, which had been prepared by the Mayor, was then read by the Town Clerk. The address is too long to be printed here, but abounded in expressions of admiration and respect for General Grant, and of welcome to the hospitalities of England. Jacob Bright, Esq., M. P. for Manchester, in expressing the hope that wherever General Grant went in England, he would receive the honor that was due him, made a graceful allusion to the fact that the General's efforts during the American war were not for personal glory but for the freedom of his country and the stability of its institutions. He also spoke of the generosity that had characterized General Grant's treatment of his vanquished adversaries, and of the magnanimous terms offered them at the close of the war and during his administration.

General Grant's responses to these addresses were singularly happy and well-timed. We have spoken elsewhere of the fact that the General's trip abroad was a revelation to his friends at home. One of the elements in which he surprised everybody—and perhaps himself as well—was in his capacity for speech-making. All remember how difficult it was during his official life to get him to say anything in public, much less to make a deliberate speech. His habitual reserve and caution controlled him, and he was noted almost as much for his silence as for his devotion to his cigar. But freed from the trials and responsibilities of official life, his reserve gave way, and he proved to be an excellent off-hand speech-maker. His utterances were marked by candor and simplicity, equalled only by their singular aptness and propriety. He never "slopped over" in his remarks, but while always frank

BEACONSFIELD CHURCH.

KEW PALACE.

Sketches in England.

WINDSOR CASTLE—FROM EATON.

HAMPTON COURT—LOOKING UP THE RIVER.

Sketches in England.

and unaffected, bore himself with admirable dignity and self-possession. Few men ever had the capacity of saying "the right thing in the right place" that General Grant showed through all his trip around the world. In the many novel and trying situations in which he was placed, he never failed to conduct himself with credit, so that his presence always added to the favorable opinions which had been formed upon his reputation. In this, as in most respects, his success was due to the strong common-sense and good judgment which are the dominant elements in his character. His unaffected earnestness and simplicity gave him the dignity and grace of a true gentleman, which the utmost efforts of more polished and artificial manners can only imitate.

In his reply to the address of the Mayor of Manchester, General Grant said:

"MR. MAYOR, MEMBERS OF THE COUNCIL OF MANCHESTER, LADIES AND GENTLEMEN: It is scarcely possible for me to give utterance to the feelings called forth by the receptions which have been accorded me since my arrival in England. In Liverpool, where I spent a couple of days, I witnessed continuously the same interest that has been exhibited in the streets and in the public buildings of your city. It would be impossible for any person to have so much attention paid to him without feeling it, and it is impossible for me to give expression to the sentiments which have been evoked by it. I had intended upon my arrival in Liverpool to have hastened through to London, and from that city to visit the various points of interest in your country, Manchester being one of the most important among them. I am, and have been for years, fully aware of the great amount of manufactures of Manchester, many of which find a market in my own country. I was very well aware, during the war, of the sentiments of the great mass of the people of Manchester toward the country to which I have the honor to belong, and also of the sentiments with regard to the struggle in which it fell to my lot to take a humble part. It was a great trial for us. For your expressions of sympathy at that time, there exists a feeling of friendship toward Manchester, distinct and separate from that which my countrymen also feel, and I trust always will feel, toward every part of England. I therefore accept, on the part of my country, the compliments which have been paid to me as its representative, and thank you for them heartily."

At Salford, on the way from Manchester to London, General Grant said at the luncheon given him by the Mayo

"My reception, since my arrival in England, has been to me very expressive, and one for which I have to return thanks on behalf of my country. I cannot help feeling that it is my country that is honored through me. It is the affection which the people of this island have for their children on the other side of the Atlantic, which they express to me as an humble representative of their offspring."

An acknowledgment of an address from the Mayor and Council of Leicester was thus briefly and happily made·

"Allow me, in behalf of my country and myself, to return you thanks for this honor, and for your kind reception, as well as for the other kind receptions which I have had since the time that I first landed on the soil of Great Britain. As children of this great commonwealth, we feel that you must have some reason to be proud of our advancement since our separation from the mother country. I can assure you of our heartfelt good-will, and express to you our thanks on behalf of the American people."

At Bedford, the Mayor waited upon the General at the train, and presented an address full of complimentary allusions, terming General Grant the Hannibal of the American armies, and hoping he might long be spared to enjoy further honors which would be heaped upon him. In replying to this enthusiastic speech, General Grant simply expressed his thanks for the Mayor's courtesy, and regretted his inability to make a speech that would compare in eloquence to those of his British friends.

There is no doubt that General Grant was deeply sensible of the marked attentions that had been shown him, and that he was greatly pleased by them. He did not, however, take all the compliments to himself, but ascribed a large part of them to the desire to express feelings of friendship for his country. This thought is shown in several of his speeches, and is so admirably expressed in a private letter written about this time to a friend in America, that the letter is well worth quoting here:

"After an unusually stormy passage for any season of the year, and continuous seasickness generally among the passengers after the second day out, we reached Liverpool Monday afternoon, the 28th of May. Jesse and I proved to be among the few good sailors. Neither of us felt a moment's uneasiness during the voyage. I had proposed to leave Liverpool immediately on my arrival and proceed to London, where I knew our Minister had made arrangements for the formal reception, and had accepted for me a few invitations of courtesy. But what was my surprise to find nearly all the shipping in port at Liverpool decorated with flags of all nations, and from the mainmast of each the flag of the Union most conspicuous. The docks were lined with as many of the population as could find standing-room, and the streets to the hotel, where it was understood my party would stop, were packed. The demonstration was, to all appearances, as hearty and as enthusiastic as in Philadelphia on my departure. The Mayor was present in his state carriage, to convey us to the hotel; and after that he took us to his beautiful country residence, some six miles out, where we were entertained with a small party of gentlemen, and remained over night. The following day a large party was given at the official residence of the Mayor in the city, at which there were some one hundred and fifty of the distinguished citizens and officials of the corporation present. Pressing invitations were sent from most of the cities in the kingdom to have me visit them. I accepted for a day at Manchester, and stopped a few moments at Leicester and at one other place. The s me hearty welcome was shown at each place, as you have no doubt seen. . . . I appreciate the fact, and am proud of it, that the attentions I am receiving are intended more for our country than for me personally. I love to see our country honored and respected abroad, and I am proud that it is respected by most all nations, and by some even loved. It has always been my desire to see all jealousies between England and the United States abated, and every sore healed. Together, they are more powerful for the spread of commerce and civilization than all others combined, and can do more to remove causes of war by creating mutual interests that would be so much endangered by war. . . .

"U. S. GRANT."

On the first day of June, four days after his landing in Liverpool, General Grant arrived in London. The scenes and events during his month's stay in the British metropolis were among the most interesting of his entire journey; and to them we shall devote a separate chapter.

CHAPTER V

HONORS OF LONDON.

General Grant in London—Character of his Reception—His Public Speeches—Advantages of Knowing but one Language—Brilliant Social Events—The "Freedom of the City."—A Pleasant Souvenir—Address of the Lord Mayor—General Grant's Response—The Grand Banquet—Some Happy Hits—The General as a Speech-Maker—Opinion of the "Tribune" Correspondent—The Guest of the Queen—Visit to Windsor Castle—A Greeting from Home—Some Distinguished Gatherings—General Grant's Talk to the Workingmen—The "Pump-handle Process"—A Familiar Experience—Courtesies from the Prince of Wales—English Journalists and Literary Men—Fourth of July in London—How the General Celebrated—A Sprightly Description by an Observer.

General Grant's visit in London was notable not only for the wonderful sights which he saw in that mighty city, but for the marked attentions which he received on every hand. The most distinguished statesmen and people known in all the various walks of fame, the highest London officials and members of the British government, as well as the Queen and the leading nobility, showed him the most flattering marks of respect and admiration. Such a reception, so generous and at the same time so hearty and cordial, was probably never before given in England to an American citizen. That General Grant was deeply sensible of the compliments paid him in these attentions, is evident from his speeches, which include the best of those made by him in his entire travels. Indeed, his speeches in London and other portions of Great Britain comprise the most of what he said in a public way; his ignorance of foreign languages being an effective excuse for silence in other countries. He remarked, jokingly, to a friend, that his ignorance of all languages but one was a great piece of good fortune to him, since it obviated any necessity for public speaking. Occasionally, it is true, he spoke through an interpreter, and at other times he met distinguished men of foreign countries who conversed readily in English, and with whom many interesting informal conversations were had, which have fortunately been preserved. But the General's English speeches are by far the most noteworthy of his recorded utterances, and will be given in full here.

The first two weeks of General Grant's stay in London were taken up by a series of social events and sight-seeings which, though full of interest, it is impossible to fully describe here without infringing upon the space needed for recording more important matters. Passing over, therefore, the visit to Epsom Downs, where the General first met the Prince of Wales, from whom he afterwards received marked attentions; the events of the three days' delightful visit to his daughter, Mrs. Sartoris, at her residence at Southampton; the continuous round of dinners and receptions given in the General's honor by the Duke of Devonshire, Lord Granville, Sir Charles Dilke, the Duke of Wellington, Lord Carnarvon, and the American Minister and Consul, and attended by the most brilliant society in London; the visit to Westminster Abbey on Sunday, where Dean Stanley made a graceful allusion in his sermon to the presence in England of an Ex-President of the United States; passing by, also, the interesting ceremonies attending the General's presentation at Court on the 7th of June, we come to one of the most noteworthy and impressive incidents of his visit, which it is impossible to dispose of without a more extended mention. This is the conferring upon the General of the "freedom of the city of London"—a very rare honor, and the highest which the corporation of London can bestow.

LONDON—THE THAMES EMBANKMENT.

ENGLAND—OLD WESTMINSTER BRIDGE.

The ceremonies attending this interesting event took place on June 15th, in the Guildhall, one of the most prominent and historic buildings in the city. The guests were eight hundred in number, including Members of Parliament, the Chancellor of the Exchequer, members of the city government, the American Minister, and many American residents of London. A great many ladies were also in attendance.

General Grant was received at the Guildhall by a deputation of the city government, who conducted him to the Council Chamber, where he was placed at the left of the Lord Mayor. The Chamberlain then read an address to the General, which is as follows:

"The unprecedented facilities of modern travel, and the running to and fro of all classes in our day, have brought to our shores unwonted visitors from Asia, as well as from Europe—rulers of Empires both ancient and of recent creation ; but amongst them all we have not as yet received a President of the United States of America—a power great, flourishing and free, but so youthful that it celebrated only last year its first centennial. A visit of the ruling President of those States is scarcely to be looked for, so highly valued are his services at home during his limited term of office; you must bear with us, therefore, General, if we make much of an Ex-President of the great Republic of the New World visiting the old home of his fathers. It is true that those first fathers—Pilgrim Fathers we now call them—chafed under the straitness of the parental rule, and sought in distant climes the liberty then denied them at home; it is true, likewise, that their children subsequently resented the interference, well intended if unwise, of their venerated parent, and manifested a spirit of independence of parental restraint not unbecoming in grown-up sons of the Anglo-Saxon stock. Yet, for all this, there is furnished from time to time, abundant evidence that both children and parent have forgotten old differences and forgiven old wrongs; that the children continue to revere the mother country, while she is not wanting in maternal pride at witnessing so numerous, so thriving, and so freedom-loving a race of descendants. If other indications were wanting of mutual feelings of regard, we should find them, on the one hand, in the very hospitable and enthusiastic reception accorded to the Heir Apparent to the British throne, and subsequently to H. R. H. Prince Arthur, when, during your presidency, he visited your country; and on the other hand, in the cordial reception which, we are gratified to observe, you have received from the hour when you set foot on the shores of Old England. In this spirit, and with these convictions, the Corporation of London receives you to-day with all kindliness of welcome, desiring to compliment you and your country in your person by conferring upon you the honorary freedom of their ancient city—a freedom which had existence more than eight centuries before your first ancestors set foot on Plymouth Rock; a freedom confirmed to the citizens, but not originated, by the Norman conqueror, which has not yet lost its significance or its value, although the liberty which it symbolizes has been extended to other British subjects, and has become the inheritance of the great Anglo-American family across the Atlantic. But we not only recognize in you a citizen of the United States, but one who has made a distinguished mark in American history—a soldier whose military capabilities brought him to the front in the hour of his country's sorest trial, and enabled him to strike the blow which terminated fratricidal war and reunited his distracted country; who also manifested magnanimity in the hour of triumph, and amidst the national indignation created by the assassination of the great and good Abraham Lincoln, by obtaining for vanquished adversaries the rights of capitulated brethren in arms, when some would have treated them as traitors to their country. We further recognize in you a President upon whom was laid the honor, and with it the responsibility, during two terms of office, of a greater and more difficult task than that which devolved upon you as a general in the field—that of binding up the bleeding frame of society which had been rent asunder when the demon of slavery was cast out. That the constitution of the country over which you were thus called to preside survived so fearful a shock, that we saw it proud and progressive, celebrating its centennial during the last year of your official rule, evinces that the task which your countrymen had committed to you did not miscarry in your hands. That such results have been possible must, in fairness, be attributed in no inconsiderable degree to the firm but conciliatory policy of your administration at home and abroad, which is affirmed of you by the resolution of this honorable Court whose exponent and mouthpiece I am this day. May you greatly enjoy your visit to our country at this favored season of the year, and may your life be long spared to witness in your country, and in our own— the two great branches of the Anglo-Saxon family—a career of increasing amity, mutual respect, and honest, if spirited rivalry—rivalry in trade, commerce, agriculture, and manufacture; in the arts, science, and literature; rivalry in the highest of all arts, how best to promote the well-being and to develop the industry of nations, how to govern them for the largest good to the greatest number, and for the advancement of peace, liberty, morality, and the consequent happiness of mankind. Nothing now remains, General, but that I should present to you an illuminated copy of the resolutions of this honorable Court, for the reception of which an appropriate casket is in preparation; and, in conclusion, offer you, in the name of this honorable Court, the right hand of fellowship as a citizen of London." (Cheers.)

The "freedom of the city," which was thus impressively bestowed, was contained in a beautiful gold casket—a most elegant and elaborate affair. At each end of the casket is a figure, in gold, representing the Republic of the United States and the city of London. The side panel contains a beautiful relief view of the Capitol at Washington, and on the reverse side is a similar view of the Guildhall, together with an appropriate inscription. Beside the panels are the monogram of General Grant and the arms of the Lord Mayor. There are double columns at the corners, entwined with laurel wreaths and leaves of corn and cotton, and surmounted by cornucopias, emblematic of the productiveness and prosperity of the United States. The casket is supported by golden American eagles standing on its base, while the cover is surmounted by the arms of the city of London, with decorations of the rose, the thistle, and the shamrock. The design and workmanship of the casket are artistic and elegant to a high degree; and General Grant may well value this beautiful gift as among the choicest souvenirs of his trip abroad.

To the Chamberlain's address, General Grant replied as follows:

"It is a matter of some regret to me that I have never cultivated that art of public speaking which might have enabled me to express in suitable terms my gratitude for the compliment which has been paid to my countrymen and myself on this occasion. Were I in the habit of speaking in public, I should claim the right to express my opinion, and what I believe will be the opinion of my countrymen when the proceedings of this day shall have been telegraphed to them. For myself I have been very much surprised at my reception at all places since the day I landed at Liverpool up to my appearance in this the greatest city in the world. It was entirely unexpected, and it is particularly gratifying to me. I believe that this honor is intended quite as much for the country which I have had the opportunity of serving in different capacities, as for myself, and I am glad that this is so, because I want to see the happiest relations existing, not only between the United States and Great Britain, but also between the United States and all other nations. Although a soldier by education and profession, I have never felt any sort of fondness for war, and I have never advocated it except as a means of peace. I hope that we shall always settle our differences in all future negotiations as amicably as we did in a recent instance. I believe that settlement has had a happy effect on both countries, and that from month to month, and year to year, the tie of common civilization and common blood is getting stronger between the two countries. My Lord Mayor, ladies, and gentlemen, I again thank you for the honor you have done me and my country to-day."

This was a capital speech, and was received with hearty cheers. But still more felicitous were the remarks made by the General at the grand banquet which followed the ceremonies in the Guildhall. In response to the toast of the Lord Mayor in his honor, General Grant said.

"MY LORD MAYOR, LADIES AND GENTLEMEN: Habits formed in early life and early education press upon us as we grow older. I was brought up a soldier—not to talking. I am not aware that I ever fought two battles on the same day in the same place, and that I should be called upon to make two speeches on the same day under the same roof is beyond my understanding. What I do understand is, that I am much indebted to all of you for the compliment you have paid me. All I can do is to thank the Lord Mayor for his kind words, and to thank the citizens of Great Britain here present in the name of my country and for myself."

That what we have said in regard to the remarkable success of General Grant as a speech-maker may not appear extravagant, we will quote from the account of this affair printed in the New York *Tribune,* and written by its accomplished London correspondent, Mr. G. W. Smalley, who was a guest upon the occasion. In describing General Grant's three speeches on that day, Mr. Smalley says:

"The first was a somewhat elaborate address in the library of the Guildhall, in response to the still more elaborate address of the Chamberlain in offering him the freedom of the City of London. It was thoroughly well done in manner and matter. The second was at the lunch at the Guildhall, and was simply a gem. I never heard a more perfect speech of its kind. There is a charm, a felicity in the turn of one or two of its phrases that would do credit to the best artists in words—to Mr. Kinglake or to Mr. Matthew Arnold themselves. Later in the day, at the quiet and almost private dinner at the Crystal Palace, Mr. Thomas Hughes asked the company, in a few words full of grace and feeling, to drink the health of General Grant. Mr. Hughes took pains to say that the occasion was not formal, and that he did not mean to impose upon his guest the burden of a reply. General Grant sat looking up into Mr. Hughes' face; there was a moment's pause, and then the General, screwing himself slowly up out of his chair till he stood erect on his feet, said: 'Mr. Hughes, I must none the less tell you what gratification it gives me to hear my health proposed in such hearty words by Tom Brown of Rugby.' I do not know what could be better than that. Still later in the evening, during the exhibition of fireworks, General Grant sat silent while his own portrait—a capital likeness—was drawn in lines of changing flame against the dark background of Beckenham Hills. Not a muscle moved; there was not a sign of pleasure at the splendid compliment paid him; not a movement of recognition for the cheers with which the great crowd below hailed the portrait. But when this had burnt out, and the next piece—a sketch of the building which crowns the heights above the Potomac—was blazing, a slight smile parted the General's lips as he remarked to Lady Ripon, who sat next to him: 'They have burnt me in effigy, and now they are burning the Capitol!'"

An interesting feature of the entertainment at the Crystal Palace, referred to by Mr. Smalley, was the execution of an overture and chorus written for the occasion by a Chicago composer,

Mr. S. G. Pratt, and performed then for the first time. Longfellow's "Village Blacksmith" was also sung by a distinguished tenor, and the bands played English and American national airs.

Another event of very great interest during the General's stay in London was the dinner with the Queen at Windsor Castle. For this memorable occasion, invitations were sent as follows:

"The Lord Steward of Her Majesty's household is commanded by the Queen to invite Mr. and Mrs. Grant to dinner at Windsor Castle on Wednesday the 27th inst., and to remain until the following day, the 28th of June, 1877."

At half-past eight o'clock on the evening of the dinner, General and Mrs. Grant were received by the Queen and her court in the State apartments of Windsor Castle, the dinner being served in the famous Oak Room. Among the guests were Prince Leopold, Prince Christian, Princess Beatrice, Lord and Lady Derby, the Duchess of Wellington, General Badeau, Mr. Pierrepont, the American Minister, and wife, and many others of prominence. The affair was a very brilliant one, and General Grant enjoyed it highly. After dinner the Queen conversed pleasantly with the General, who was delighted with his informal chat with her and other members of the royal family.

An interesting episode of this occasion was the receipt by General Grant of the following dispatch from an army re-union in America:

"PROVIDENCE, RHODE ISLAND, June 27, 1877.
"*From General Hartranft, Commander in Chief, to General U. S. Grant, care of H. R. M. the Queen:*
"Your comrades in National Encampment assembled in Rhode Island, send heartiest greetings to their old commander, and desire, through England's Queen, to thank England for Grant's reception."

This dispatch was given by General Grant to Her Majesty, who expressed her pleasure at the greeting. The General at once telegraphed this response:

"Grateful for telegram. Conveyed message to the Queen. Thank my old comrades."

General Grant and family spent the night at Windsor Castle, in accordance with the invitation of the Queen, and the next morning returned to London.

A great many other dinners and receptions were given the General in the city, which we would like to describe in full, but can do little more than mention. The entertainments given in his honor by the Prince of Wales at Marlborough House, where the General met the Emperor of Brazil, with whom he became on very friendly relations; the dinners with Lord Ripon and Lord Derby at their residences, and with the Princess Louise and the Marquis of Lorne at the Kensington Palace; the visit to the venerable Earl Russell at Richmond Park;—all these were highly interesting and memorable occasions. So

E

also was the dinner at the United Service Club, at which the Duke of Cambridge presided, where General Grant met some of the most distinguished officers of the British Army and Navy, including the Admiral of the Fleet, Sir George Sartorius. There was no speech-making on these occasions, as they were essentially private and informal in their nature.

A very neat and sensible speech was, however, made by General Grant on an occasion of another sort, about this time, in response to an address presented to him by the Workingmen's League of Great Britain, a deputation of which waited upon him at the house of Gen. Badeau. It was as follows:

"GENTLEMEN: In the name of my country I thank you for the address you have just presented to me. I feel it a great compliment paid to my Government, to the former Government, and one to me personally. Since my arrival on British soil I have received great attentions, and, as I feel, intended in the same way for my country. I have received attentions and have had ovations, free hand-shakings, and presentations from different classes, and from the Government, and from the controlling authorities of cities, and have been received in the cities by the populace. But there is no reception I am prouder of than this one to-day. I recognize the fact that whatever there is of greatness in the United States, or indeed in any other country, is due to the labor performed. The laborer is the author of all greatness and wealth. Without labor there would be no government, or no leading class, or nothing to preserve. With us labor is regarded as highly respectable. When it is not so regarded it is that man dishonors labor. We recognize that labor dishonors no man; and no matter what a man's occupation is he is eligible to fill any post in the gift of the people. His occupation is not considered in the selection of him, whether as a lawmaker or an executor of the law. Now, gentlemen, in conclusion, all I can do is to renew my thanks to you for the address, and to repeat what I have said before, that I have received nothing from any class since my arrival on this soil which has given me more pleasure."

The address was received with great satisfaction by the deputation, after which they indulged in a general "hand-shaking" with the General—a process which must have reminded him forcibly of some of his American experiences while holding "President's receptions" at the White House.

A grand banquet was given the General on the evening of June 22d, by the Trinity Corporation, at their hall, at which the Prince of Wales, who presided, said:

"It is a matter of peculiar gratification to us as Englishmen to receive as our guest Gen. Grant. I can assure him for myself and for all loyal subjects of the Queen, that it has given me the greatest pleasure to see him as a guest in this country."

To this complimentary allusion, as well as to that made by Lord Carnarvon, Secretary of Home Affairs, General Grant responded briefly and gracefully, thanking the gentlemen for their kindness, and expressing the most cordial sentiments of reciprocity. Among the many distinguished persons in this brilliant company were Prince Leopold, Prince Christian of Schleswig-Holstein, the Prince of Leiningen, Prince Edward of Saxe-Weimar, the Duke of Wellington, the Earl of Derby, and others.

Not the least important of all these social occasions was the breakfast given General Grant by Mr. Smalley, the London correspondent of the New York *Tribune*, at his handsome residence in Hyde Park Square, at which some of the most notable literary men of England were present—including Robert Browning, Matthew Arnold, Kinglake the historian, Trollope the novelist, Prof. Huxley, Thomas Hughes, and many others. This was a famous gathering, and gave a pleasant variety to the society of eminent statesmen and members of the nobility, from whom General Grant had received such distinguished consideration. So, also, was the dinner given at the Grosvenor House on the 29th, where the General met many of the leading journalists of the city; of which Mr. Smalley wrote to the New York *Tribune:* "General Grant himself—who must by this time rank as an expert in such matters—pronounces this dinner one of the most enjoyable of the many given him in London." All the prominent English journalists were present, as were some from this side of the water.

The last social ceremonies attended by General Grant previous to his departure from London were a reception and dinner at the American Embassy on the Fourth of July. They were a fitting close to the continuous and brilliant festivities that had marked the General's visit, and are so admirably described by Mr. Smalley in a letter to the New York *Tribune* that we perhaps cannot do better than make some extracts from his account:

"The Fourth of July was observed in London at the Legation, and so far as I know at the Legation only. The papers announced that the Minister of the United States and Mrs. Pierrepont would receive Americans from four to seven in the afternoon, General Grant and Mrs. Grant to be present. The Americans presented themselves in large numbers. It is the season when a good many of our countrymen are in London, on their way to the Continent, and not a few such birds of passage thronged the rooms of the Legation yesterday afternoon. Of resident Americans there were also many—so many that I won't undertake to repeat their names. And there was a pretty large sidewalk committee outside, attracted by the American flag which floated over the doorway, and by the carriages setting down company—the latter always a favorite sight with the poor devils who spend their days in the street. Whether because it was the great Saint's Day of America, or of any other equally good reason, a vast deal of what is called good feeling is shown—a degree of cordiality in the greetings between acquaintances greater than might be expected when you consider that these same people live three-fourths of the year or more in the same town and within a few miles of each other, but are seldom on intimate terms. There are no dissensions to speak of among Americans here (though there have been), but neither is there much gregariousness. Patriotism got the upper hand yesterday, however. The lion and the lamb took tea together—nay, dined together later. Pretty girls abounded. The American girl is always pretty, or, at least, always expected by the Briton to be pretty. The Briton was not there yesterday to see how many of them there were. California contributed its quota; Boston and New York were not unrepresented; Baltimore sent a belle or two, and there were ladies no longer to be called girls who might have disputed with the best of their younger sisters for the palm of beauty. I think I noticed in my fellow citizens a slight uncertainty as to the sort of costume that ought to be worn on so solemn an occasion. The white tie was prematurely seen—it was only five o'clock in the afternoon, and your true Englishman never wears it before dinner, and dinner is never before eight—and some dress coats covered the manly form. I don't think I saw any ladies without bonnets. General Grant arrived a little late, and till he came nobody went away, so that the crush in Mr. Pierrepont's spacious rooms was for some time considerable. General and Mrs. Grant held a levee whether they would or no; their admiring and eager countrymen and countrywomen swarmed about them. Once more the General might have fancied himself in the White House, judging by the severity of the 'free hand-shakings' he underwent. Not a man or a woman of those who gathered about spared him, nor did he flinch; but we dare say he reflected with pleasure that he was going to countries where hand-shaking is much less in fashion than here or at home.

"Last of all, the General dined, on the evening of the 4th, at the Legation of the United States. The occasion was not made a very ceremonious one; with a single exception, only Americans were put on guard that night. The exception was Monsignor Capel. The dinner was so far informal and private that I hardly know whether I am right in saying anything about it. Most of the distinguished Americans known to be passing through London were invited, and were present. The list included Senator Conkling, Governor Hendricks, Judge Wallis of the United States District Court—the same who lately tried the Emma Mine case—the Rev. Phillips Brooks of Boston, and Chancellor Remsen of New Jersey. Mrs. Grant and Mrs. Pierrepont were the only ladies present. The evening was a very pleasant one, and was greatly enjoyed by all. As the General proposed starting next day for a short run to the Continent, the guests departed at an early hour, wishing the party a pleasant trip through Belgium and Switzerland."

CHAPTER VI.

ON THE CONTINENT.

General Grant's Method of Journeying—"Traveling at Will"—Leaving London—Crossing the Straits of Dover—Arrival at Ostend—A Welcome to Belgium—A Ride in the King's Car—At Brussels—Meeting with King Leopold—The Sovereign and the Citizen—Up the Rhine—Cologne, Weisbaden, Coblentz, Frankfort—In a German *Palmer Garten*—Baden, Hamburg, and the Black Forest—A German Journalist interviews General Grant—His views of Military Events and Men in America—In Switzerland—Interesting Events at Geneva—Among the Alps—The Lakes of Northern Italy—Towards England—Alsace and Lorraine.

In the progress of his journey, General Grant did not follow rigidly any pre-determined route, after the conventional guide-book method, but left a good deal to varying taste and inclination, and to the changing circumstances of time and season. When weary of one country, or feeling inclined to a change of scenery, he did not compel himself to remain till he had seen all that he wished or intended to, but would if necessary return and complete the visit at another time. He did not take in order all the countries that lay before him, after the manner of a traveling drummer who must visit all the places on his particular route, but went here and there as his mood or convenience suited, and often visited the same country or region more than once. This is the true method of the traveler who has time and means for it, since it leaves him far more free, and avoids any danger of monotony by giving a constant variety of scenery and experience. In this narrative, therefore, which is designed as a record of General Grant's personal travels rather than a description of the countries and places visited by him, we shall pursue the same method which the General adapted in his journeyings, and go here and there among the countries of the earth in the by indirect fashion which the General followed in his trip around the globe.

At the time when our last chapter closed, General Grant had by no means completed his visit in Great Britain; but before finishing it he decided to relieve his month's continuous stay in London, and the somewhat arduous hospitalities showered upon him there, by a short run to the Continent—leaving the remainder of England, as well as Scotland and Ireland, for a later period.

On the morning of July 5th, the General and Mrs. Grant, accompanied by their son and General Badeau, left London and took passage across the Straits of Dover for Ostend—a ride of about 150 miles. A change of country did not, however, lessen the kind and thoughtful attentions with which the General was everywhere received. On landing at Ostend he was immediately waited upon by an officer sent by the Belgian King to tender the party the use of the royal car for the journey to Brussels. After listening to a congratulatory address from the civil and military authorities of Ostend, where they passed the night, the party left the next morning for Brussels, stopping on the route to visit briefly the ancient and curious city of Ghent, with its quaint buildings and belfry towers.

At Brussels the General received many flattering attentions, but the most interesting feature of his visit there was his meeting with King Leopold of Belgium, and the friendly intimacy which sprung up between him and that distinguished sovereign. The King is a man of marked ability and high character, and his intelligent conversation, and especially his familiarity with American affairs, made a most favorable impression upon the General; while the King was in his turn greatly pleased with the character of his distinguished visitor. There was a fine contrast presented in these two men—one a royal sovereign of an ancient line, ruling for life and by the "divine right of Kings;" the other, a man of wonderfully varied fortune, called from the humblest pursuits of private life to become the great military hero of his century, then chosen by the people to be the President of the greatest Republic in the world, and now simply a private citizen again, traveling for his own purposes of pleasure and information. But striking as was the contrast in their histories and positions, they were quick to recognize in each other the qualities of genuine manhood which both respected. and through which they became firm and appreciative friends. They had many long and interesting conversations together, King Leopold calling upon the General at his hotel, and the General and Mrs. Grant returning the visits at the royal palace. The evening before their departure from Brussels, the King entertained them at a banquet at his palace, at which were gathered, as on that fatal evening before the battle of Waterloo, the "beauty and the chivalry" of Belgium's capital.

On the morning of July 9th General Grant and party left Brussels in the King's railway carriage, and proceeded to the famous city of Cologne, on the historic River Rhine. The General spent only a day at Cologne, and proceeded up the Rhine to Weisbaden and Coblentz;—at each city receiving formal offerings of respect from the civil and military authorities. At Frankfort, where he arrived on the 12th of July, the American residents of the city had arranged a grand banquet and *fete* in his honor. It was given in the *Palmer Garten* in the evening; and at the conclusion of the feast, when the General attempted to take a stroll with his cigar through the famous gardens, he found them occupied by a throng of perhaps ten thousand people, who had come to catch a sight of the American general. Other dinners and receptions, and visits to the many interesting objects in the neighborhood, occupied the three days spent in Frankfort; and on the 15th the party went to Heidelberg. Brief visits to Baden, to Hamburg, and to the celebrated Black Forest, completed for the present the tour of Germany.

The following very spicy and entertaining gossip connected with General Grant's German visit is given by a Hamburg correspondent, writing under date of July 20, 1877:

"Ex-President Grant arrived here July 18th. In conversation the General gave his views about the American war and its Generals. Among other things he said that if he had known the soldiers and Generals of the Potomac any better, he would have preferred to invest Lee in Richmond from Lynchburg on the land side as he invested Pemberton at Vicksburg. He says his total losses in the Wilderness campaign amounted to only thirty-nine thousand men. He says General Butler wishes he had abler subordinates and expresses regret that an unlucky phrase in his official reports should have annoyed Butler. He thinks Jefferson Davis did all he could for the confederacy, and did not deserve the harsh criticisms he got. He thinks Stonewall Jackson might not have proved so effective a General later on in the war, and opposed to men like Sherman and Sheridan, when his peculiar tactics would have failed. He seems to think Lee not so great as his reputation; speaking of him, of course, as a soldier, and not as a man. He was never so uneasy when in front of Lee as some other commanders, and he describes him as a man slow of mind, without imagination, and great dignity of demeanor. General Joe Johnston, in his opinion, was the ablest commander on the southern side. Of Bragg he appears to have had but a poor opinion.

"General Grant tells a singular story of President Johnson's device at one time to arrest General Lee and other southern commanders for treason by way of making rebellion odious. Grant and Seward had, it appears, the means and good sense to oppose and defeat this folly, and General Grant says he would have resigned his command rather than to have consented to the arrest of Southern men, they being sacred under their parole to him.

"Rosencranz, Buckner, McClellan, Buell, Stoneman, and McDowell, he says, were in the opinion of the old army, the more promising officers in 1861. He still thinks Buell had genius for the highest commands, and McDowell was a man of great ability, and he cannot account for the ill luck of poor Stoneman, whom he knew as one of the most highly cultivated officers in the old army, and one of the best soldiers. Hancock, he thinks, one of the ablest of our Generals.

"Sherman and Sheridan he praised without stint. He related an old story of his first meeting with the la ter when Sheridan, then Colonel of a regiment, was rude to him. Sherman, he says, is not only one of the best men living, but one of the greatest we have in our history, and he gives a curious account of how Sherman's narrative of the war was misrepresented to him, so that he determined to read it, pencil in hand, and publish a reply, but found it a true book, an honorable book, just to all, and he approved every word of it.

"General Grant says he did not want to go to West Point, never liked a command, and remonstrated against the creation of the grade of Lieutenant General made for him, though he saw the necessity for it later. He dispelled some romances of the war, as where he says, there was no battle of Lookout Mountain, no action worthy to be called a battle. He says neither he, Sherman nor Sheridan ever held a council of war. He determined on his course in private, and no one knew what he was about to do until orders were written out.

"Finally he speaks about his Presidential career. He thinks the second term was almost his due, because he had been bitterly opposed, but relates how he refused a third nomination, which was urged upon him on the ground that the contest would belittle him; that if re-elected, it would only have been against strong opposition, and his administration of a third term would have been unsatisfactory."

On the 24th of July the General arrived at Berne, in Switzerland, from whence he went to Geneva. At the latter place, on the 27th, there were some very interesting ceremonies connected with laying the corner-stone of a new Episcopal church, built by the American residents of Geneva,—General Grant himself laying the corner-stone. After these exercises, there was a banquet at the hotel, at which the General, in response to the warm welcome extended to him, declared that he "had never felt himself more happy than among this assembly of fellow Republicans of America and Switzerland." He added: "I have long had a desire to visit the city where the Alabama Claims were settled by arbitration without the effusion of blood, and where the principle of international arbitration was established, which I hope will be resorted to by other nations and be the means of continuing peace to all mankind."

The first half of the month of August was spent by General Grant among the grand scenery of the Alps. The visit to Mont Blanc was made memorable by an illumination in the General's honor, which produced a magnificent effect. The General enjoyed immensely his rambles among the Alpine ranges, and by the beautiful lakes of Northern Italy; and after resting a few days at Ragatz, to enjoy the wonderful baths of that celebrated place, the party proceeded by easy stages back toward England. The route lay through Alsace and Lorraine—a country of special interest to the General, from the memorable battles fought there between the French and Germans. He showed himself thoroughly familiar with the events of the recent war between those nations; and his visit to the scenes where so many of those events transpired was reckoned by General Grant as among the most instructive and satisfactory of his two months' trip upon the Continent.

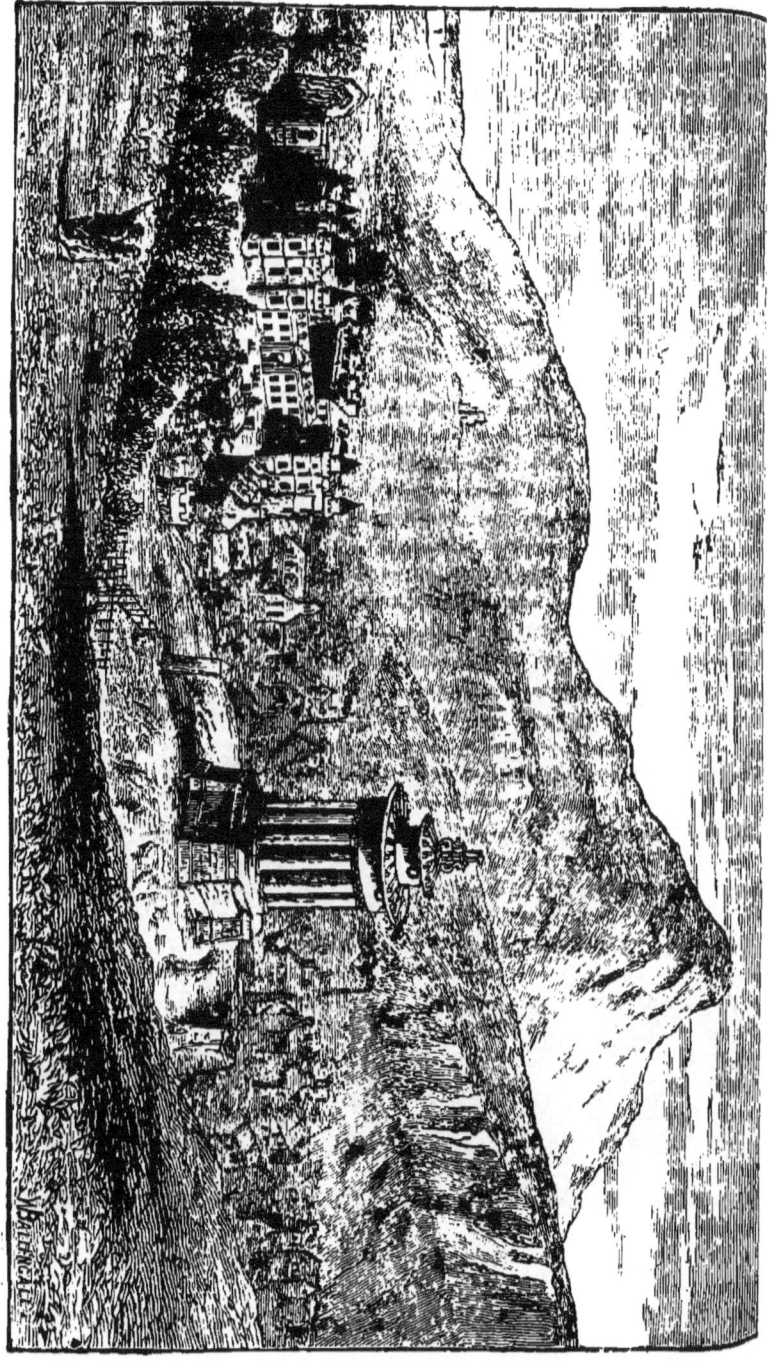
EDINBURGH.—HOLYROOD AND BURNS MONUMENT.

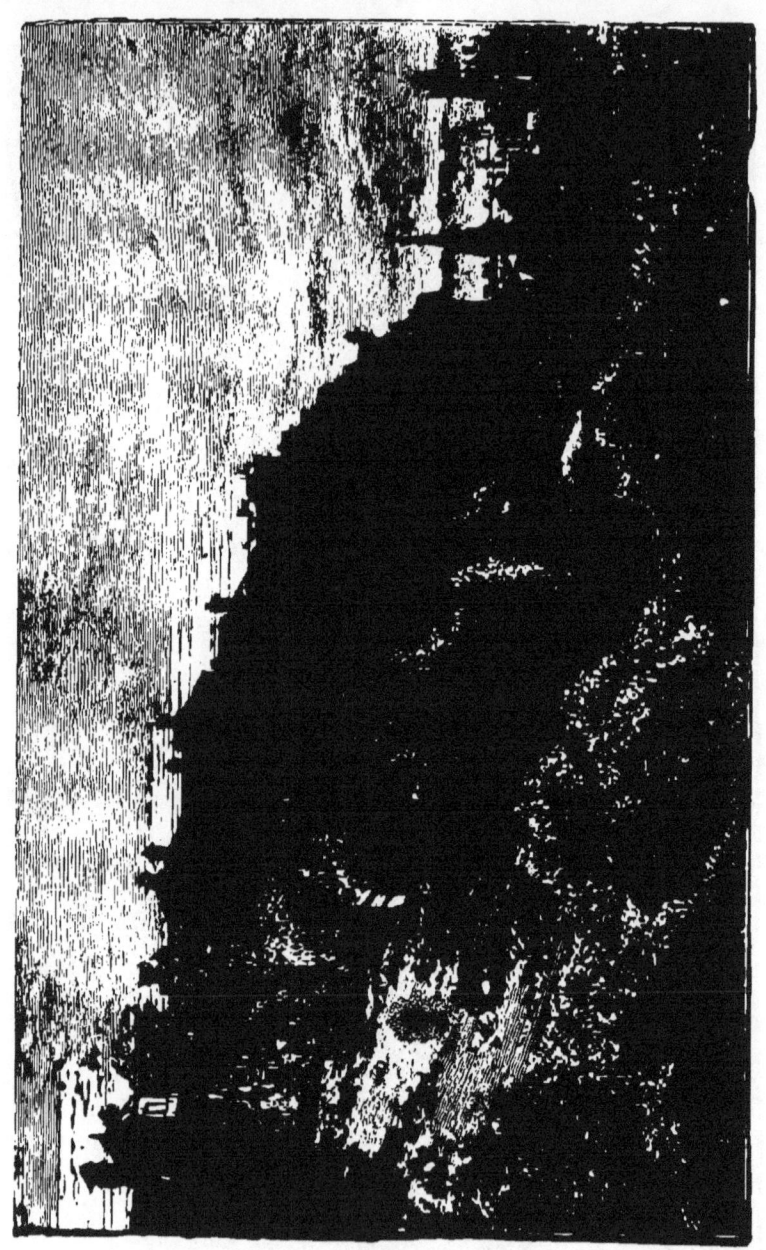

EDINBURGH—THE CASTLE AND ALLAN RAMSAY'S HOUSE.

CHAPTER VII.

SCOTLAND, THE HOME OF THE GRANTS.

Re-Crossing the English Channel—From London to Edinburgh—Freedom of the City—Scottish Hospitality—A bit of Scotch Humor—In the Highlands—The "Grant Clan."—At Granttown—The General's Speech at Wick—Arrival at Glasgow—A Grand Ovation—General Grant the "Wellington of America"—A Notable Speech by the General—He Frees His Mind on the Alabama Award, for the Benefit of a Scotch M. P.

The first real halt made by General Grant after re-crossing the channel from his Continental trip was at the fine old city of Edinburgh. All along the road from London he was met with lavish honors and attentions, but time would not permit anything more than the briefest stops at the stations on the way. He reached Edinburgh on the last day of August, 1877. The interesting ceremonies of a presentation of the freedom of the city were here repeated, on a scale only less magnificent than in London. More than two thousand people, including the most distinguished persons in the place, gathered in the Free Assembly Hall, where, in reply to the presentation speech of the Lord Provost, Gen. Grant said:

"I am so filled with emotion that I scarcely know how to thank you for the honor conferred upon me by making me a Burgess of this ancient City of Edinburgh. I feel that it is a great compliment to me and to my country. Had I the proper eloquence, I might dwell somewhat on the history of the great men you have produced, on the numerous citizens of this city and of Scotland who have gone to America, and the record they have made. We are proud of Scotchmen as citizens of America. They make good citizens of our country, and they find it profitable to themselves. I again thank you for the honor conferred upon me."

The neat humor of his reply produced much laughter and good feeling. Every one was delighted with the General, and all were desirous of showing him kind attentions and making his stay in Scotland as agreeable and profitable as possible. Especially interesting was the visit to the Scottish Highlands, where a well-known and ancient clan bear the Grant name, and from whom the General is supposed to have descended.

At Granttown, near Inverness, the General was appropriately welcomed to the "Home of the Grants," and near by is Castle Grant, the home of the Earl of Seafield, the present head of the Grant clan in Scotland.

The ceremony of conferring the "freedom of the city" was repeated at every considerable place which General Grant visited in Scotland. One of the happiest speeches made by him in reply to presentation addresses on these occasions was at the provincial but not unimportant town of Wick, where the General spoke as follows:

"I am happy to state that during the eight years of my Presidency it was my only hope, which I am glad to say was realized, that all differences between the two nations should be healed in a manner honorable to both. In my desire for that result it was my aim to do what was right, irrespective of any other consideration whatever. During all the negotiations, I felt the importance of maintaining friendly relations between the great English speaking peoples, which I believe to be essential to the maintenance of peace principles, and I feel confident that the continuance of those relations will exercise a vast influence in promoting peace and civilization throughout the world." [Great applause.]

Gen. Grant reached Glasgow on the 13th of September, where he received a grand and enthusiastic ovation. At the City Hall, in the presence of an immense multitude, he was presented with an address in which the City Council "admitted and received General Ulysses Simpson

Grant, ex-President of the United States of America, to be a Burgess and Guild Brother of the City and Royal Burgh of Glasgow, in recognition of his distinguished abilities as a statesman and administrator, his successful efforts in the noble work of emancipating his country from the horrors of slavery, and of his great services in promoting commerce and amity between the United States and Great Britain." To this complimentary address the General replied simply and happily, remarking that he had been so many times made a citizen of Scotland that it might become a serious question where he should go to vote. Several other addresses were made on this memorable occasion at Glasgow, in one of which, by the Lord Provost of the city, General Grant was felicitously alluded to as "the Wellington of America"—an allusion which called out tremendous cheering, which was renewed when the speaker added that "the great and good Lincoln struck down the upas tree of slavery, but Grant tore it up by the roots so that it should never live again in his country."

One of the most extended and notable speeches made by Gen. Grant during his entire trip was made upon this occasion, when, in answer to one of the speakers—a member of Parliament—who had remarked, with rather questionable taste, that in view of the dissatisfaction of Great

Britain with the Geneva Award, and the fact that the United States had completed the distribution of the award and had some $8,000,000 left after all claims had been satisfied, he would be pleased to see the government return that amount in the interests of concord and thorough amity. The General replied that he had a great deal to do with the negotiations concerning the Washington treaty, and that he had always felt that our Government had yielded too much to Great Britain in the matter. He was determined, however, from the first, that, if possible, the experiment of peaceful arbitration should prevail. It was his ambition to live to see all national disputes settled in this way. "I am called a man of war," said he, "but I never was a man of war. Though I entered the army at an early age, I got out of it whenever I found a chance to do so creditably. I was always a man of peace, and I shall always continue of that mind. Though I may not live to see the general settlement of national disputes by arbitration, it will not be very many years before that system of settlement will be adopted, and the immense standing armies that are depressing Europe by their great expense will be disbanded, and the arts of war almost forgotten in the general devotion of the people to the development of peaceful industries. I want to see, and I believe I will, Great Britain, the

United States and Canada joined with a common purpose in the advance of civilization, an invincible community of English-speaking nations that all the world beside could not conquer." The General continued in this vein for some time, and presently touching the Alabama-claims question again, said: "There was one point in connection with that matter that I was glad we yielded—that was the indirect damage claim. I was always opposed to it, because I feared the future consequences of such a demand. In any future arbitration we would have been placed at a great disadvantage by its allowance. After that was settled we made our other demands, you made yours. It was a long time before the Joint High Commission came together, but each side yielded here a bit and there a bit, until about as good a treaty as we could expect to get was completed. Mr. Anderson says many of the people of Great Britain believe we got the best of the bargain. I can assure you that we did not come out of the discussion as much benefited as we should have been. Many of our people were quite incensed, and fought the confirmation of the treaty, claiming that its terms were not broad enough to cover the losses of local interests, but a very large majority determined to stand by it in the interests of peace and manly dealing with friends. We yielded more than we intended to yield, but had gone so far into the business of doing what we advocated that nine-tenths of our people had no desire to recede. We did not want war, or even a new arbitration. We had been satisfied with the former, and the latter meant delay. We wanted the question settled peacefully, at once and forever. As to the eight million surplus Mr. Anderson mentions, I will explain that briefly. After the fifteen million dollars awarded at Geneva was paid by Great Britain, the matter of its distribution was presented to Congress. It became necessary to distribute it under the terms of the treaty, and it was found that if the insurance companies which had received war premiums were admitted to participation in the sum, it would not be large enough to go around. So they and other parties were excluded. Congress will legislate further in the matter, and the money will be distributed to rightful claimants, so that it will not be necessary to discuss the question of returning it to Great Britain."

CHAPTER VIII.

AMONG THE ENGLISH WORKINGMEN.

Newcastle's Greeting—The Mayor's Welcome and the General's Response—At Tyneside—The Alabama Claims and International Arbitration — "Swingeing" Cheers — English Working People During our War—Their Sympathy with the North—At Sheffield—Banquet by the Cutlers' Company—Some Pleasant Reminiscences — Stratford-on-Avon—Visit to Nellie at Southampton—More Addresses—Slavery Discussed—At Birmingham — A Magnificent Greeting—Several Notable Addresses by General Grant—His Views on Free Trade—Speech at Brighton—What he thinks of the Volunteer System—Return to London.

General Grant took with him from Scotland the most pleasant and lively memories of his visit to that country, and on the 20th of September arrived at the famous manufacturing city of

Newcastle, on the Tyne. Here, and among the other great manufacturing districts of the North of England, he spent about a month; and nowhere was his reception more striking. The General's distinguished position as a representative of republican government, and his well-known sympathy with the cause of the people, had aroused the interest of the working classes in his visit; and the enthusiasm and cordiality with which they greeted him are almost impossible to describe. We can note only the leading incidents of what was a grand and continuous ovation, ending only with his departure from the country.

At Newcastle, where the General remained some days, he was the guest of the Mayor, Sir William Armstrong. The day after his arrival, an address was delivered to him by the Vice-President, Council, and members of the Newcastle and Gateshead Incorporated Chamber of Commerce, which referred to the natural riches and industries of the Tyne district—iron in all its branches, chemicals, lead, copper, earthenware, fire-bricks, colors and coals. "The various branches of the iron trade," said the address, "include melting the ore into pig iron, the manufacture of all kinds of wrought iron, rails, machines, ordnance, and the building of iron vessels, for which our river is famous. The shipment of coal from the town exceeds 7,000,000 tons per annum, and the number of vessels annually leaving the river, engaged in the coal trade, or loaded with the produce of our manufactories, is larger than the number leaving any other port in the world." In his reply, the General said:

"The president in his remarks has alluded to the personal friendship existing between the two nations—I will not say the two people, because we are one people (Applause); but we are two nations having a common destiny, and that destiny will be brilliant in proportion to the friendship and co-operation of the brethren on the two sides of the water. (Applause.) During my eight years of Presidency, it was my study to heal up all the sores that were existing between us. (Applause.) That healing was accomplished in a manner honorable to the nations. (Applause.) From that day to this feelings of amity have been constantly growing, as I think; I know it has been so on our side, and I believe never to be disturbed again. These are two nations which ought to be at peace with each other. We ought to strive to keep at peace with all the world besides (Applause), and by our example stop those wars which have devasted our own countries, and are now devastating some countries in Europe."

Following the exercises at the Chamber of Commerce, an excursion was had upon the river, —the party being greeted by the music of bands, the firing of rockets and cannon, and the cheers of thousands of working people along the river banks. At Tyneside they disembarked; and here the General, in response to an address complimenting him on his "valor and sagacity in battle and his clemency in victory," remarked that he "had seen that day on the banks of the Tyne no fewer than one hundred and fifty thousand people, mostly workmen, who had left their occupations and homes to manifest, as he felt it, their friendship for their grandchildren—he would not call them their cousins—on the other side of the Atlantic. He did not agree with the Mayor or member of Parliament who had spoken, in referring to the river as an insignificant one. It was true in America they had some large streams, but their greatest industries were carried on on the small streams. They had not one stream in America as yet that could show the number of industrial pursuits that the Tyne showed between Newcastle and the point at which they were now standing."

On the following day a grand demonstration of workingmen, in honor of General Grant, took place in Newcastle. There was a huge procession, composed of representatives of all the various trades and industries of Northern England, carrying appropriate banners and devices. General Grant delighted the people by riding in the procession to the town moor, where an address was delivered by Mr. Burt, M. P., on behalf of the workingmen—the crowd around the platform being estimated at 80,000. The speaker prefaced his address by some excellent and timely remarks regarding the friendship of the British working classes toward this country during our civil war. He said that there "was never a war in which English armies were not employed that went so directly to the popular feeling. This was not merely because their kinsmen were in mortal combat; but because it was a battle for great principles. It was not a war for conquest, for selfish aggrandizement, or for the propping up of a tottering throne; but it involved the great questions of freedom, of the rights of man, and the dignity and honor of labor." The speaker then congratulated America on the abolition of slavery, upon the pacific tenor of General Grant's Administration, and upon the settlement of the Alambaaio laims as one of the grandest moral victories ever achieved by statesmanship. "When the history of the nineteenth century comes to be written," said he, "one of its brightest pages will be that which tells how two of the greatest and most valorous nations of the world settled their differences by arbitration rather than by an appeal to the power of armies." Mr. Burt concluded by saying that the working people regretted that so much of the wealth, energy and intellect of the world were devoted to destructive purposes. "These huge standing armies," he said, "are a menace to peace and a constant drain on the life and resources of nations. In the face of these armies, the two great branches of the Anglo-Saxon race have before them a noble mission. If England and America, acting on the wise counsel so well given by you yesterday at the meeting of the Chamber of Commerce, strive not only to keep peace between themselves but also to keep at peace with other nations, they will set an example that was never more needed than now, and that will be rich in benefits to the whole world in all coming time."

The formal address, though long, is too important a document to be omitted here. It was handsomely bound and engrossed, and is as follows:

"GENERAL: In the name of the working classes of Northumberland and Durham, we welcome you to Tyneside, and we are proud of the opportunity afforded us of expressing to you our admiration for the noble deeds which have made you famous in the history of your country, and the welcome guest of Englishmen.

"At the outbreak of the American civil war, when called upon by your country to defend its honor and wipe from its character the stain of slavery, we are mindful that you entered upon that work with prompt zeal and unfailing fortitude; and we are sensible that the courage which sustained you during that dark period of American history, was not the courage which enables a soldier merely to face death, but that nobler courage which springs from a consciousness of duty.

"In those hard-fought battles, in which your great abilities as a soldier were displayed, and which won for you the absolute confidence of that pure and noble-minded martyr, Abraham Lincoln, you had the entire sympathy of the working classes of England; and we are all the more proud on that account in honoring you to-day as a faithful and distinguished son of America—a splendid soldier and a wise and prudent statesman.

"Though you are skilled in the art of war, we are pleased to regard you as a man of peace; but the peace which commands your sympathy must be founded on the eternal laws of equity and justice. The rough scenes of war have no charms for you; but we believe if duty called you would be ready to strike again for the consecration of noble principles.

"General, you are imperishably associated with the glorious issue of the American civil war, and posterity will assign you a conspicuous place on the roll of the world's heroes. Mankind will not forget that you have caused the 'Stars and Stripes' to float more proudly than ever over the Republic, and we rejoice to know that our kinsmen have testified their gratitude by twice electing you to the highest office in the United States. We, who are bound to them by a relationship which no circumstances can sever, join them in a grateful recognition of your services.

"Again, we welcome you as a most successful statesman, in whose custody the honor and interests of a noble nation were safely intrusted.

"The onerous duties which devolved upon you on your accession to the Presidency of the United States could not have been so ably discharged had you possessed less coolness, courage, and tenacity of purpose; and we greet you with sincere esteem for pursuing a conciliatory and peaceful policy toward this country, especially during the consideration of the difficulties between England and America.

"The terrible consequences which might have resulted to both countries had you adopted a hostile policy are harrowing to contemplate, and we are glad to know that you so largely contributed to the preservation of peace and the amicable settlement of the Alabama question.

"History will chronicle the proceedings at Geneva as a grand achievement of civilization, and with it, you, General, will ever be identified. In favoring the principle of international arbitration you have earned the applause of the civilized world, and we readily acknowledge the great blessings which that mode of settling the difficulties of nations has already conferred on your country and ours.

"It has cemented us more firmly together in the bonds of peace and friendship, and we are sure that no one is more desirous than yourself that the people of England and America, who are of one blood, and whose interests are identical, should draw more closely together, so that the future history of the two nations may be one unbroken concord.

"And now, General, in our final words we greet you as a sincere friend of labor. Having attested again and again your deep solicitude for the industrial classes, and having also nobly proclaimed the dignity of labor by breaking the chains of the slave, you are entitled to our sincere and unalloyed gratitude ; and our parting wish is, that the general applause which you have received in your own country, and are now receiving in this, for the many triumphs which you have so gloriously achieved, may be succeeded by a peaceful repose, and that the sunset of your life may be attended with all the blessings that this earth can afford.

"General, we beg of your acceptance of this address as a testimony of the high regard and admiration in which you are held among the working people of Northumberland and Durham."

To this very kind and complimentary address, General Grant made a fit and equally cordial reply. Amid tremendous cheering, the General said:

"MR. BURT AND WORKINGMEN: Through you, I will return thanks to the workingmen of Tyneside for the very acceptable welcome address which you have just read. I accept from that class of people the reception which they have accorded me, as among the most honorable. We all know that but for labor we would have very little that is worth fighting for, and when wars do come, they fall upon the many, the producing class, who are the sufferers. They not only have to furnish the means largely, but they have, by their labor and industry, to produce the means for those who are engaged in destroying and not in producing. I was always a man of peace, and I have always advocated peace, although educated a soldier. I never willingly, although I have gone through two wars, of my own accord advocated war. (Loud cheers.) I advocated what I believed to be right, and I have fought for it to the best of my ability in order that an honorable peace might be secured. You have been pleased to allude to the friendly relations existing between the two great nations on both sides of the Atlantic. They are now most friendly, and the friendship has been increasing. Our interests are so identified, we are so much related to each other, that it is my sincere hope, and it has been the sincere hope of my life, and especially of my official life, to maintain that friendship. I entertain views of the progress to be made in the future by the union and friendship of the great English-speaking people, for I believe that it will result in the spread of our language, our civilization, and our industry, and be for the benefit of mankind generally. (Cheers.) I do not know, Mr. Burt, that there is anything more for me to say, except that

I would like to communicate to the people whom I see assembled before me here this day how greatly I feel the honor which they have conferred upon me." [Cheers.]

The Newcastle paper, the *Chronicle*, devoted twenty columns the next day to an account of this affair; and as in many respects it was one of the most noteworthy incidents of the General's trip, perhaps we cannot do better than append a few extracts from the *Chronicle's* spirited report:

"A few minutes to four o'clock a general craning of necks and faint strains of music in the distance heralded the advance of the procession. Everybody tried to look over everybody's shoulder, and the unregenerate boot which always selects that precise moment to impress upon its neighbor's foot the fact that man is a pedal animal, commenced its vocation. A swingeing cheer swept up the turnpike and round the corner of the Bull Park, firing like a train of cartridges the whole of the crowd up to the platform. 'He was coming,' that was enough. So everybody cheered again, and got its lungs into lustiest order, ready for the time when the procession should actually arrive and the first captain of the Republic be visible. Like some long nondescript monster, with a dorsal fin of variegated colors, the procession slowly wormed its way up from the road in the direction of the platform. Banners flapped as banners only do flap when there is not only something in the wind, but something in men's hearts as well. Brass bands did their best to rise to the height of a great occasion, and magnify the dignity both of Apollo and of Mars. The big drum—and there might be a score in the procession—which may always be depended upon to raise enthusiasm to fever heat, led off gusty rounds of cheers, which finally eddied and swirled in splendid vociferousness. The first section of the procession halted at the east end of the platform. On any other occasion, perhaps, the silver emblems of all the Christian graces carried by the National Independent Order of Odd Fellows would have excited attention; but the top of the Mayor's carriage could be seen, and in a minute or two a vision of plush breeches and a confused rush told that the General had arrived. At this moment the crowd, with the adroitness which is always the mark of genius, and having waited until the General was on the field to appreciate the boldness of their campaign, executed a flank movement into the reserved square in front of the platform. They had been, not ill-naturedly though, chafing for hours at the idea of having the whole front of the proceedings partially hidden from them by a forest of banners; and once the attention of the police was directed to the arrival of the visitor of the day, they made a dash for the coveted position. As helpless as straws in a storm tide, the few policemen on duty were carried forward with the first lines of the crowd. For an instant, perhaps two, these front ranks were alone in the open. Then with flattering unanimity of imitation, which always animates that acute observer the public, forty thousand brains were struck by the thought that the nearer the platform the better the sight. Like the bursting of floodgates, away the mighty masses of faces came on, three huge and solid banks, rather than waves of humanity, reeling in front of the platform with a good, thorough, old-fashioned crush.

"And sooth to say it was a crush. From here and there in the fierce press came the shouts and screams of frightened lads, whose faces, reaching no higher than the waistcoat pockets of their fathers, were perforce pressed into that accommodating, but not the less suffocating, part of the mortal temple which the monks of Mount Athos considered the center of feeling. Still good-naturedly, although butted in a manner not conducive to assist digestion, a general effort was made by the men to extricate the youngsters. They were at once, with sundry rips in sundry coats, hauled up from their unseen position and literally rolled over the heads of the crowd, to be finally dropped down inside a railed-off space in front of the platform, where stout barriers kept off the crush. By this time everybody was fully occupied, partly in cheering, partly in protecting their ribs from the pressure of the crowd, partly in helping to bundle these living bales over to the platform, but chiefly in taking a good long inspection of the General. Looking as much like an ordinary Tyneside skipper as possible, open-browed, firm-faced, bluff, honest, and unassuming, everybody at once settled in his own mind that the General would do. The cheers became warmer and warmer as that quiet, strong, thoroughly British face grew upon them; and as they increased, General Grant, who had at first merely touched his hat to the multitude, bared his head, as an unmistakable everybody-joins-in-it 'Hurra' roared out from fifty thousand throats, and rattled up to the astonished birds circling overhead. But business is business, even in demonstrations, and must be attended to. The Mayor waits to open proceedings, General Grant to the right of him, and Mr. Burt to the left. Behind and around the three, who occupy the middle of the platform, are grouped the friends and leaders of industrial Northumberland and Durham; faces which have been familiar to the workers of the North for the last quarter of a century. Since the General first arrived a wonderful increase has taken place in the crowd, which now extends far on either side of the platform, stretching away in front of it to a point where even the voice of Hector would be unheard. Only part of the band has nearly reached the position intended for the section it is connected with, and apparently the little knot of crimson tunics wish themselves well out of the squeeze. One hapless individual, burdened with the care of a French horn big enough to do duty for a monster cornucopia, is at his wits' and to preserve his own bones and those of his instrument. Finally he lifts it on his shoulder, the mouth pointing toward the platform, and looking like a cross between the brass trunk of a metal mammoth and a novel weapon of war. The unfortunate processionists, elbowed so summarily out of their places, have been meantime seeking to establish themselves on the outskirts of the crowd, where, to tell the truth, they are far better situated than if they had occupied the places originally intended for them. Their banners, disposed partially around one side of the crowd, have a particularly pretty effect, hemming in the scene with a zone of color. Behind, in the far distance, may be seen, rising through the gray smoke, Newcastle's spires and steeples. Beyond these the dark hills of Gateshead close round, looking, as they seem to drop down in the soft shadow and undulation from the long bar of sunlight stretched, a golden rod, above them, as if they were hung, a stupendous curtain, worked with raised broidery of houses and churches.

"But the Mayor has commenced to speak, and following him comes Mr. Burt. The crowd, which has not got over the excitement yet, keeps up a loud hum, varied, though it cannot hear a word of what is said, with occasional cheers, by way of expressing its conviction that the member for Morpeth is saying the right thing in the right place. When Mr. Burt takes the blue-bound address in his hand they cheer it, and break out into still more sonorous exclamations when General Grant receives that expression of the interest Tyneside labor has taken in his visit. The last of the procession, however, has not yet arrived on the ground, and the music of distant bands, swelling in with the restless stir of the crowd, prevents any but a few on the platform from expecting to hear what reply the Ex-President will make. Seeing the state of matters he addresses himself to the reporters, delivering, for him, an unusually long speech, and speaking with an evident feeling which shows that the crowd, as is nearly always the case with men who have handled large bodies of men, has touched his sympathies. The vast concourse, still rushing up from the turnpike, and which now musters at least eighty to a hundred thousand, estimate the unheard speech after their own thoughts, and applaud every now and again with might and main. When the General finishes, everybody who has not yet shouted feels it incumbent to begin at once, and those who have bellowed themselves hoarse make themselves still hoarser in their endeavors to come up to the demands of the situation. Hats are waved with a self-sacrificing obliviousness to the affection subsisting between crown and brim which is beautiful to witness. And right in the center of the crowd, little shining rivulets glistening on his ebony cheeks, and his face glowing with intense excitement, the whole soul within him shining out through his sable skin like a red-hot furnace seen through a dark curtain, stands a negro, devouring Grant with a gaze of such fervid admiration and respect and gratitude that it flashes out the secret of the great liberator's popularity."

The grand festival at Newcastle, which is here so effectively described, closed with a banquet in the evening. Many good speeches were made and toasts offered—in response to one of which, offered in his honor, General Grant said:

"MR. MAYOR AND CORPORATION OF NEWCASTLE: I scarcely know how to respond to what has been said by the Mayor. I have a very vivid recollection that immediately upon my arrival upon these shores the Mayor invited me up here, and we have been carrying on a correspondence, directly and indirectly, ever since as to the time when I should be here. But as to my saying anything after I came, such a thing never occurred to me (Laughter.) I will say that the entertainment by your worthy Mayor has exceeded my expectations. I have had no better reception in any place, nor do I think it possible to have a better. (Cheers.) All I have seen since I have been on the Tyne has been to me most gratifying as an individual, and I think when I go back to my own country I will find that it has been very gratifying to my countrymen to hear of it. It has been gratifying all along the Tyne to Tynemouth. It has been gratifying because I have seen that which is extremely pleasant, namely, the good relationship existing, that should always exist, between English-speaking people. (Applause.) I think that is a matter of the vastest importance, because I believe that we have the blessings of civilization to extend. I do not want to detract from other civilizations; but I believe that we possess the highest civilization. There is the strongest bond of union between the English-speaking people, and that bond should and will serve to extend the greatest good to the greatest number. That will always be my delight."

An exceedingly interesting feature of this banquet was the reference made to the position of England during our civil war, and to the well-known friendship for the North felt by English working people. In touching upon this topic, Mr. Cowen, M. P., spoke with great earnestness and candor. He said:

"General Grant's achievements would fill a large and glowing page in the history of his native land, and no inconsiderable one in the history of our times. His position as a soldier and a statesman was fixed, and there was not now time, and this was not the occasion, to dilate on it. He had won the confidence of his contemporaries and secured the encomiums of posterity. The world has often spoken with admiration of his valor and his resolution—of his courage and ability, He had no wish to underrate or overlook these virtues; but to-night he would speak of his modesty and magnanimity. He knew of nothing more touching than the gentleness with which General Grant conveyed a necessary, but at the same time a hasty and unpleasant command, from the American War Minister to his brave companion-in-arms, General Sherman, nor more generous than his dignified treatment of the vanquished Confederate captain—a foeman worthy of his steel. These actions reminded us of the fabled days of chivalry. The only incident in modern warfare to be compared to them was the conduct of our own manly Outram toward the gallant Havelock on the eve of the fate of Lucknow. On the questions involved in the great conflict in which our illustrious guest played so decisive a part, there were wide differences of opinion amongst us. We all followed his career with interest and with admiration—many of us, most of us in this district with sympathy. The different views existing in English society found memorable expression on two occasions in Newcastle. In the midst of the war, at a banquet in our town hall, Earl Russell gave it as his opinion that the North was fighting for empire and the South for independence. Mr. Gladstone, the year after, in the same place and on a like occasion, declared that the South had made an army, were making a navy, and would make a nation. He referred to these statements not for the purpose of reviving a long-forgotten and exhausted controversy, nor with the object of pointing out that the 'common people,' when great principles were at stake, were often right when statesmen, who took a technical view of the struggle, were in error. But he recalled the circumstances because it was but meet that the people of Tyneside, who did not share the sentiments of these two Liberal statesmen, should seize the opportunity of a visit from the great Republican commander to 'cull out a holiday,' to climb to walls and battlements, to towers and windows, to greet the man who fought and won the greatest fight for human freedom that this century has seen. Lord Russell, with characteristic courage and candor, not long after he made his speech in Newcastle, declared that he had misapprehended the objects of the American war, and acknowledged he had been wrong in the views he had entertained. Mr. Gladstone was scarcely so ready and frank with his recantation, but he also ultimately confessed that he had not understood the purposes of the Republican leaders. He trusted that General Grant's visit to this country would prevent a repetition of such misconceptions, would help to draw still closer the bonds of unity between America and England, and tend to prevent the bellicose spirits in both nations plunging us into suffering and confusion for the gratification of unworthy and antagonistic passions. Our common interests were peace. We were streams from the same fountain—branches from the same tree. We sprang from the same race, spoke the same language, were moved by the same prejudices, animated by the same hopes; we sang the same songs, cherished the same liberal political principles, and we were imbued with the conviction that we had a common destiny to fulfill among the children of men. We were bound by the treble ties of interest, duty and affection to live together in concord. A war between America and England would be a war of brothers. It would be a household martyrdom only less disastrous than war between

Northumberland and Middlesex. The pioneers of the Republic—the Pilgrim Fathers—were pre-eminently English. It was because they were so that they emigrated. They left us because England in that day had ceased to be England to them. They went in the assertion of the individual right of private judgment and the national right of liberty and conscience. They carved out for themselves a new home in the wilderness, into which they carried all the industrial characteristics and intelligent energies of the mother land. They did not leave us when England was in her infancy. Our national character was consolidated before they went, and Shakespeare and Milton and Bacon, and all the great men of the Elizabethan era, were not only figuratively but literally as much their countrymen as ours. They repudiated the rule of the English king, but, as they themselves declared, they never closed their partnership in the English Parnassus. They would not own the authority of our corrupt court, but they bowed before the majesty of our literary chiefs. They emigrated from Stuart tyranny, but not from the intellectual and moral glories of our philosophers and poets, any more than from the sunshine and dews of heaven. These literary ties had been extended and strengthened by years. The names of Longfellow and Lowell, Bryant and Whittier, were as much household words with us as those of Campbell and Coleridge, Byron and Burns, Dickens and Thackeray. Bulwer and Jerrold wrote as much for America as for England. The works of Hawthorne and Cooper, Emerson and Irving, came to us across the sea bathed in the fragrance of their boundless prairies, redolent of the freshness of their primeval pine forests, and were read and admired as warmly on the banks of the Tyne and the Thames as on the shores of the Potomac and the Mississippi. But in addition to the intellectual, there were strong material ties intertwining the two nations. When the United States ceased to be part of the English dominions, an increased commercial intercourse sprang up between us. Coincident with the close of the American War of Independence, the ingenuity and skill of our countrymen led to the discovery of those great mechanical inventions which produced the cotton trade. While the spindles of the Lancashire mill-owners had been weaving wealth for themselves and power for their country, they had bound in a web of interest and good-will the American planter and merchant and the English manufacturer and workman. They trusted that when their distinguished guest returned home, he would assure his fellow countrymen that there was amongst men of all classes, sects and parties in England, only one feeling toward America, and that was one of friendship—that we had only one rivalry with her, and that was to excel in the arts of peace and the works of civilization."

Such are the more prominent features of the General's visit to Newcastle, though many minor details are necessarily omitted. At Sheffield, another famous manufacturing town, the reception was no less cordial and impressive. Arriving on the 26th of September, the party were welcomed by the Mayor and city officials, and a complimentary address was read, to which General Grant made this response:

"Mr. Mayor, Ladies and Gentlemen of Sheffield : I have just heard the address which has been read and presented to me, with great gratification. It affords me singular pleasure to visit a city the name of which has been familiar to me from my earliest childhood. I think the first penknife I ever owned, away out in the western part of the State of Ohio, was marked 'Sheffield.' I think the knives and forks we then used on our table had all of them 'Sheffield' marked on them. I do not know whether they were counterfeit or not, but it gave them a good market. From that day to this the name of your industrial city has been familiar, not only in the States, but I suppose throughout the civilized world. The city has been distinguished for its industry, its inventions, and its progress. If our commerce has not increased as much as you might wish, yet it has increased, I think, with Sheffield since the days of which I spoke when we had no cutlery excepting that marked 'Sheffield.' It must be very much larger than it was then. We are getting to make some of those things ourselves, and I believe occasionally we put our own stamp upon them; but Sheffield cutlery still has a high place in the markets of the world. I assure you it affords me very great pleasure the welcome that I have received here to-day, and I shall carry away with me the pleasant recollections of what I have seen in Sheffield."

An address from a society of Sheffield cutlers, in which reference was made to the subject of free trade, brought out the following manly and felicitous reply from the General:

"Mr. Master Cutler and Gentlemen of the Society of Cutlers: After the few remarks I made in reply to the address of the Mayor there is hardly anything for me to say further than that I feel gratified, highly gratified, at this reception. In the matter of free trade, I would hardly be able to speak upon that subject without some preparation. It must be recollected, however, that the country which I had at one time the honor of representing has gone through a great war and contracted a great debt in suppressing a rebellion. That makes it necessary to raise a large amount to support the running expenses of the Government, and to pay the interest on the debt which is owing to foreign countries to a very large extent. It is impossible to raise these revenues from internal sources. The protective tariff is a matter scarcely heard of now in the United States, though it was a common subject of talk years ago. The reason it is scarcely mentioned now is that the revenue from imports is regarded simply as one of the means of raising the necessary money to pay the interest upon the National debt and the other expenses incident to the carrying on of the Government, and if we were to abolish the revenue from imports, the foreign bondholders would very soon cry out against us because we failed to pay the interest on the bonds which they hold. (Laughter.) We get along rapidly enough in that direction, and we will compete with you in your manufactures in the markets of the world. The more of your merchants and mechanics that go to America, the better. Nothing pleases us more than the immigration of the industry and intelligence of this community. We have room for all, and will try to treat you as you have treated me to-day."

While in Sheffield, General Grant visited the celebrated Rogers Cutlery Works, and also some immense rolling-mills, where he witnessed the operation of rolling a twenty-five ton mass of iron. This interesting and exciting scene is thus described by the Sheffield *Telegraph:*

"On the furnace doors being opened only those whose eyes are accustomed to the scene could view anything within it beyond a white mass of burning material. A crane traveling overhead, however, carried a pair of huge tongs to the mouth of the furnace; they were thrust within it, and with the help of the engines the heap of seething metal was drawn forth upon an iron lurry. The heat in the mill was now tremendous, and the majority of the strangers were endeavoring to shield their eyes from the blinding glare of the material, and at the same time seeking to protect their faces from the heat. The lurry was hastened to the rolls,· and at the first passage a shower of fire was ejected as the iron ran through; at the same time the dross running from the sides of the plate as whey does from a cheese. In eight minutes, after being several times passed and repassed through the gigantic rolls, the operation was concluded. As the General left the mill he was again heartily cheered, a second compliment, which he again acknowledged. The derrick for testing rails was shown in operation. A section was placed beneath it, and a weight of one ton drawn to a height of twenty-five feet above it, when it was allowed to fall. The rail, however, only bent, and showed no sign of fracture. The operation of converting Bessemer steel was next witnessed. When the party reached this department, one of the huge 'receivers' was just ready to be charged with the iron. The blast was put on, and for twenty minutes the party had an opportunity of viewing at close quarters a display which it would be difficult for any pyrotechnist to imitate. Now and again as some mass of slag was driven high into the air, and fell back upon some damp place in the pit, an explosion would ensue, which must have reminded the General of the bursting of shell. This process appeared to excite the attention of the ladies most of all, and when at last the operation of converting was completed, and an adjournment was made to a cooler place, it was with no small amount of relief to many, the heat being almost insupportable. In the planing-room it was explained how the armor plates are dressed into presentable form, how they had bolt holes drilled through them, and how the port holes were cut out. In this apartment were exhibited two plates which had been subjected to experiments at Shoeburyness. They were manufactured of iron, with a surface of steel, under a process patented by Mr. Alex. Wilson. Although only nine inches thick, no shot had been able to pierce through them. The bending of a section of an eight-inch plate, cold, was perfectly successful, no flaw of any description being found on the piece after this severe test."

At the grand banquet held in the famous hall of the Cutlers' Company, in Sheffield, one of the speakers, Mr. Mundella, M. P., made this happy reference to a visit made by him to America and to his meeting with General Grant while the latter was President:

"I was in Washington, and was introduced by one of the Ministers of Gen. Grant's Government to the President of the Republic—Gen. Grant himself. We had some conversation about the speeches and about the references that had been made to the relations between the two countries. The words which the General spoke were few, brief, weighty and encouraging, and were in favor of peace with England. And he encouraged me and Mr. Hughes to go on in the same direction as had some of the most prominent men in America—the best spirits in the country; and, gentlemen, should it ever be your lot, as it has been mine, to sit down at Boston, and there to meet the literary men, the poets, and the statesmen of America, depend upon it you will be prouder of the Anglo-Saxon race from that time forth than you are to-day. I say these men were of one mind and one heart, that between the brothers on this side of the Atlantic and the brothers on the other side there should be peace, hat all sources of quarrel should be removed. When I came home I went to Lord Granville and Mr. Forster, and they sent me to Mr. Gladstone. I placed before them all I had heard and seen in America, and humble though my part may have been, I am proud to have been even one of the humblest instruments in the formation of some measures and the confirmation of negotiations which produced that great international understanding between the two nations, which is to the lasting honor of Mr. Gladstone's Government. Mr. Forster said to me this morning as he came down with me in the train on his way to Bradford, that we all ought to be grateful to Gen. Grant, as during his Presidency he was the confirmed friend of peace with England, and that he would not allow any political faction to trade upon war with England, and thereby to make political capital out of such a criminal cry."

In reply to a toast to the health of General Grant, proposed by the Mayor, the General responded:

"MR. MAYOR, AND LADIES AND GENTLEMEN OF SHEFFIELD: It makes my heart feel glad when I hear these sentiments uttered in regard to my own country, and to the friendship which should exist between the two nations. As I have had occasion to say frequently, it has always been a cherished view of mine that we should be the best of friends. I am sure, as an official in a position that gave me some little power of healing the little grievance that was caused between the two nations, I exercised all the influence I had to bring about a settlement that would be a final settlement, as I believed—and I believe now that it is a final settlement. It was not a question of whether we should get this or that, it was simply a question of whether we should agree; it was not a matter of dollars and cents—they were entirely unnamed as compared with the question of a settlement. Our wish was simply to have a settlement—that both parties should agree and settle the matter. We have agreed upon terms, and I believe that this is the beginning of a long series of years—I hope centuries—of friendly and honorable rivalry between the two great English-speaking nations and the advancement of each. Whatever tends to the advancement of one in some way or another will tend to the advancement of the other."

General Grant's visits to the celebrated manufacturing towns of northern England, where he found so much to interest him, were pleasantly relieved at this time by a short trip to Stratford-on-Avon, and by a few days spent in the quiet and repose of his daughter's beautiful home at Southampton. Going thence to Leamington, a large and pleasant town, he was met by the Mayor and other officials, who, in their address, adverted to the war for the abolition of slavery in America, and to the prominent part taken in it by General Grant. "It was a memorable day for your country," said the Mayor, "and a great day for humanity at large, when, by the efforts of Abraham Lincoln and yourself, aided by the enlightenment of the American people, slavery was forever abolished from your land." The General made a happy and (for him) lengthy response, saying:

"MR. MAYOR, LADIES AND GENTLEMEN OF LEAMINGTON: It is a source of great pleasure to me to visit your renowned borough. It is a place well known by the citizens of my own country. Two of my children have visited you much earlier than I ever found time to do myself, and have carried home with them most pleasurable recollections, not only of what they saw in Leamington, but of the very kind treatment which they received at the hands of some of your citizens. I have no doubt you have many places of interest surrounding your city, only a few of which I shall be able to visit during the short stay I shall be able to make here; but I shall take home some pleasurable recollections of my visit. I am sure that it affords me great gratification to see the number of people who are outside to receive me as the representative of a kindred people. I know the feeling of friendship between the two great English-speaking nations is strengthening day by day and year by year, and I have no doubt but that, in the future, all our differences being amicably and fairly adjusted, we shall go hand in hand as honorable rivals in producing what is necessary for the comfort and support of men; and that our united efforts will be felt throughout the civilized world, and will have a beneficial effect in carrying a better civilization. I hope that through our influence we may be able at some future day to settle questions of difference without resort to arms. Although it has been my misfortune to have been engaged in as many battles as it was possible for an American soldier of my generation, I never was for war, but always preferred to see questions of difference settled by arbitration. But in our last great conflict there was the institution of slavery. It was not a conflict between two nations—it was a family quarrel; and there was no way of settlement. Every honorable effort was made on the part of the North to avoid war. We know as a people—though, perhaps, it is not generally known—at all events, it is not generally spoken of—that our martyred President, when he saw that conflict was inevitable, proposed to the South that they should be paid for their slaves if they would surrender them, and come

H

back into the family circle. But this they refused, and the result was, as you all know, the loss of that species of property without compensation."

Before leaving this part of England, General Grant made the visit to Birmingham which he had promised on a previous occasion. His reception here was one of the most magnificent which he received in England. Arriving at Birmingham, October 10th, he was taken to the Town Hall, where, in response to the Mayor's address, the General said:

"MR. MAYOR, LADIES AND GENTLEMEN: It is with great pleasure that I find myself in Birmingham, a city that was so well known in my own country during the trying periods that have been referred to. The name of the distinguished gentleman who has represented you for so long, is as familiar almost in my own country as it is in his own home, and I can promise that if it ever should be his good pleasure to visit the United States—and I hope it will—he will receive as hearty a welcome as it has been my privilege and pleasure to receive at the hands of the English communities I have been among. Your city and its growth are also somewhat familiar to us. The connection between this city and the United States has been as intimate almost as any other city of the same population in the kingdom; and there is a warm feeling of fellowship between our citizens and the citizens of Birmingham. As I have had occasion so repeatedly to express my views on the importance of this subject, I need scarcely say anything more than to thank you, Mr. Mayor, and the citizens of Birmingham, for the kind reception I have received at your hands, and to apologize to you for having kept you waiting here so long."

An address on behalf of the industrial classes of Birmingham, congratulating America on the abolition of slavery, and upon having established arbitration as a principle of international peace, was thus happily responded to by the General:

"WORKINGMEN OF BIRMINGHAM: I have just heard your address with great interest. I have had occasion twice before, I believe, since I have been in England, to receive addresses from the workingmen of Great Britain—once in London and once in Newcastle-on-Tyne. In my response, on both occasions, I expressed what I thought was due to the workingmen, not only of my country and of Great Britain, but to the workingmen all over the world. I said that we in our country strove to make labor respectable. There is no class of labor that disqualifies a man from any position, either in society or in official life. Labor disgraces no man; unfortunately you occasionally find men disgrace labor. Your Mayor has alluded to the fact that the population of Birmingham had tripled itself in fifty years. I would ask the Mayor whether, if Birmingham had been deprived of its handicraft laborers, it would have seen any such increase? It is due to the labor and to the manufacture of articles which are turned out by the means of labor, that you have grown in population and wealth. In response to the kindly feelings which exist between the workingmen of Birmingham and those of the United States, and the compliments you have paid to me for the efforts I have made in the cause of freedom and the North, I thank you most heartily."

In another address on this occasion, allusion was made to Gen. Grant's efforts as President to ameliorate the condition of the Indians by the appointment of commissioners from the Society of Friends. "Our hearts," said the speaker, "have also been deeply touched by your just and beneficent treatment of the colored freedmen. You guided them in their faltering steps as they marched out of bondage; you defended them from their enemies; you cared for them in their distresses; you aided them in obtaining education; and you claimed for them their rights as citizens; and now 'the blessing of him that was ready to perish shall come upon you, for you delivered the poor that cried, and the fatherless, and him that had none to help him.'" In reply, General Grant said:

"MEMBERS OF THE MIDLAND INTERNATIONAL ARBITRATION UNION: I thank you for your address. It is one that gives me very little to reply to, more than to express my thanks. Though I have followed a military life for the better part of my years, there was never a day of my life when I was not in favor of peace on any terms that were honorable. It has been my misfortune to be engaged in more battles than any other general on the other side of the Atlantic; but there was never a time during my command when I would not have gladly chosen some settlement by reason rather than by the sword. I am conscientiously, and have been from the beginning, an advocate of what the society represented by you, gentlemen, is seeking to carry out; and nothing would afford me greater happiness than to know, as I believe will be the case, that, at some future day, the nations of the earth will agree upon some sort of congress, which shall take cognizance of international questions of difficulty, and whose decisions will be as binding as the decision of our

Supreme Court is binding on us. It is a dream of mine that some such solution may be found for all questions of difficulty that may arise between different nations. In one of the addresses, I have forgotten which, reference was made to the dismissal of the army to the pursuits of peaceful industry. I would gladly see the millions of men, who are now supported by the industry of the nations return to industrial pursuits, and thus become self-sustaining, and take off the tax upon labor which is now levied for their support."

At the grand banquet at the Birmingham Town Hall, the Mayor contrasted the career of General Grant with that of the First Napoleon—both being great soldiers, but while the efforts of the latter had been directed toward undermining the institutions of his country, those of the former had been directed solely toward his country's peace and prosperity. In responding to this high compliment, General Grant said:

"MR. MAYOR, LADIES AND GENTLEMEN OF BIRMINGHAM: I scarcely know how to respond to a toast which has been presented in such eloquent language, and in terms so complimentary to myself and to the nation to which I belong, and in which I have had the honor of holding a public position. There are some few points, however, alluded to by your representative in Parliament, that I will respond to. He alluded to the great merit of retiring a large army at the close of a great war. If he had ever been in my position for four years, and undergone all the anxiety and care that I had in the management of those large armies, he would appreciate how happy I was to be able to say that they could be dispensed with. (Laughter and applause.) I disclaim all credit and praise for doing that one thing. I knew that I was doomed to become a citizen of the United States, and, so far as my personal means went, to aid in eradicating the debt already created, and in paying my share of any expenses that might have to be borne for the support of a large standing army. Then, further, we Americans claim to be so much of Englishmen, and to have so much general intelligence, and so much personal independence and individuality, that we do not quite believe that it is possible for any one man there to assume any more right and authority than the Constitution of the land gave to him. (Hear, hear.) Among the English-speaking people we do not think these things possible. We can fight among ourselves, and dispute and abuse each other, but we will not allow ourselves to be abused outside; nor will those who look on at our little personal quarrels in our own midst permit us to interfere with their own rights. Now, there is one subject that has been alluded to here, that I do not know that I should speak upon it at all; I have heard it occasionally whispered since I have been in England—and that is, the great advantages that would accrue to the United States if free trade should only be established. I have a sort of recollection, through reading, that England herself had a protective tariff until she had manufactories somewhat established, I think we are rapidly progressing in the way of establishing manufactories ourselves; and I believe we shall become one of the greatest free-trade nations on the face of the earth; and when we both come to be free-traders, I think that probably the balance of nations had better stand aside, and not contend with us at all in the markets of the world. If I had been accustomed to public speaking—I never did speak in public in my life until I came to England—I would respond further to this toast; but I believe that the better policy would be to thank you not only for the toast, and the language in which it has been presented, but for the very gratifying reception which I have had personally in Birmingham."

Leaving Birmingham on the 20th of October, the General made a brief visit to Brighton, where he delivered his last English speech. It was on the occasion of a grand banquet in his honor, on the 22d of October, when, in response to the Mayor's toast to his health, General Grant said:

"MR. MAYOR AND GENTLEMEN: I have to rise here in answer to a toast that has made it embarrassing to me, by the very complimentary terms in which it has been proposed. But I can say to you all, gentlemen, that since my arrival in England, I have had the most agreeable receptions everywhere; and I enjoy yours exceedingly. In a word, I will say that Brighton has advantages which very few places have, in consequence of its proximity to the greatest city in the world. There you can go and transact your business, and return in the evening. If I were an Englishman, I think I should select Brighton as a place where I should live, and I am very sure you could not meet a jollier and better people anywhere. But I would say one word in regard to a toast which preceded, and that is in regard to your Forces. I must say one word for the Volunteers, or Reserve Forces, as I believe you call them. They are what the English-speaking people are to rely on in the future. I believe that wherever there is a great war between one civilized nation and another, it will be these Forces in which they will have to place their confidence. We English-speaking people keep up the public schools in order to maintain and advance the intelligence of our country, and, in time, fit our people for volunteer service, and for higher training; and you will always find the men among them who are equal to any occasion. I have forgotten a good deal our Mayor has said that I would like to respond to, but I can say, that since I landed in Liverpool, my reception has been most gratifying to me. I regard that reception as an evidence of the kindest of feeling toward my country, and I can assure you, if we go on as good friends and good neighbors, that the English-speaking people are going to be the greatest people in the world. Our language is spreading with greater rapidity than the language of any other nation ever did, and we are becoming the commercial people of the world."

Leaving Brighton, General Grant proceeded at once to London, where he arrived October 23d. He was highly pleased with his visit to the great industrial regions of England, and had nothing but pleasant memories of his reception and experience there.

SCENE IN A BURIAL GROUND.

TURKISH QUARTERS—STAMBOUL.

Sketches in Constantinople.

NEAR CORTINA.

UNKONA MOUNTAIN, NEAR CORTINA.

Sketches in Austria.

CHAPTER IX.

PARIS.

Among the French—In the Home of Marshal MacMahon—Greeted by Minister Noyes—Six Weeks in the City of Luxuries—At the Exposition.

Up to the present point of our narrative, the travels of General Grant and party had been, with the exception of his flying trip up the Rhine and across the Alps to Italy, among English-speaking people. He was now to bid adieu to those countries where his native tongue was the prevailing language, and for the remainder of his journey around the globe—excepting only his brief visit to Ireland (to be spoken of in its proper place in these pages)—he was to hear English only with a foreign accent, or among his fellow-travelers from his own country or from England. So great is the diffusion of the Anglo-Saxon tongue in these modern times, that there is little danger of going where it is unknown; but still it is a new and somewhat startling sensation to the traveler, when he finds himself in countries where all the native population speak in language unintelligible, or at least unfamiliar, to his ears.

The General's visit to Paris had already been postponed longer than had been expected, and on the 24th of October, the day after his return from the manufacturing districts of England, he left London, accompanied by Mrs. Grant and their son, and proceeded by special train to Folkstone, where they took a steamer and crossed the English Channel. On landing at Boulogne the party were met by the prefect of the department, who welcomed them to the soil of France in the name of Marshal MacMahon, the President. Stopping only a few hours at Boulogne, a train took them thence to Paris, a hundred and fifty miles away.

The General's reception at the French capital was hearty and enthusiastic. Before reaching the Paris depot the train was met by the American Minister, General Noyes, the French Consul-General Torbert and an aide-de-camp of President MacMahon, who welcomed General Grant as an ex-President of the Republic of the United States in the name of the President of the French Republic. Leaving the train, the General and party made their way through the immense crowd gathered at the depot to receive them, and were driven at once to the Hotel Bristol.

The General remained in Paris about six weeks. The visit there was a very pleasant and interesting one, devoted mainly to the ordinary round of sight-seeing, varied by occasional banquets and receptions, and to an exchange of civilities on a high official scale. There was, however, on these occasions but little speech making. What there was, was mainly of a formal character, the General contenting himself with a brief exchange of courtesies, and a simple acknowledgment of the kindness and compliments tendered him. The presentation to Marshal Mac Mahon was an exceedingly interesting episode. The meeting between these illustrious military heroes, resembling each other not only in soldierly qualities, but in having been called by the people to the chief magistracy of the countries which they had served as soldiers, was very cordial on both sides, and was repeated many times during General Grant's stay in Paris. The General also met Gambetta, the great republican leader; the Count of Paris; Emile Girardin, whom Horace Greeley once said was the greatest journalist in the world; Rochambeau, Lafayette, Edmond About, Labonlaye, and many other of the foremost men of France. The American Minister, Gen. Noyes, did all in his power to add to the pleasure of Gen. Grant's stay in Paris. Several receptions were given at the residence of Gen. Noyes, and by the American colony in Paris, which were attended by nearly every American in the city. In the midst of such attention and hospitalities as these, and with a constant succession of sight-seeing among the varied and endless objects of interest with which Paris abounds, the time passed rapidly; and it was the 13th of December before the General was ready to continue his journey. The American man-of-war "Vandalia," then cruizing in the Mediterranean, having been kindly placed at his disposal by our Government, the party proceeded to Villefranche, where the vessel was awaiting them, and embarked for Italy and the Orient. The General visited Paris again in the following Spring, but his stay was then brief and uneventful—the only important occurrence being the visit to the French Exposition.

CHAPTER X.

ITALY AND THE MEDITERRANEAN.

Along the Mediterranean—The "Vandalia" at Naples—At Pompeii—King Humbert to Grant—Florence, Pisa and Palermo—Christmas on Shipboard—Off for Egypt.

General Grant and family had already, in their brief trip to Switzerland in July and August, crossed the Alps and made a hasty visit to the lovely lake region of Northern Italy. Their subsequent travels included visits to all the principal Mediterranean cities and places of interest—Naples, Mount Vesuvius, Pompeii, Rome, Florence, Venice, Milan, Palermo, and Malta. The first port entered by the "Vandalia" with her distinguished passengers was Naples, in whose beautiful bay the vessel anchored on the 17th of December, 1877. General Grant at once went ashore and made a brief tour of the city. The weather was cold and disagreeable, and the sights of Naples were not specially interesting. The next day the party made the ascent of Mount Vesuvius, and on the following day visited Pompeii. The General showed the keenest interest in these wonderful ruins, with their historic memories and sublime relics of the past. He remarked that Pompeii "was one of the few things which had not disappointed his expectations, the truth being far more striking than imagination had painted it; and that it was well worth a journey over the sea to see these stately and solemn ruins." In honor of the General's visit to Pompeii, the authorities directed that a house be excavated in his presence—a compliment paid only to the most distinguished visitors, and one which had already been shown to Generals Sherman and Sheridan on the occasions of their visit there. The results of the excavation for the benefit of General Grant were the discovery of a few bronze ornaments and a loaf of bread wrapped in cloth, which were removed from the dust and ashes which had overwhelmed them seventeen centuries ago, and carefully preserved as souvenirs.

It had been the plan of General Grant, somewhat jaded with the too-abundant hospitalities of Great Britain and Paris, to pursue his Mediterranean travels nearly incognito. He desired more to see the scenery and the people than to be lionized or to meet distinguished officials; and accordingly he sought to travel like a private citizen, burdened as little as possible by official attentions and formalities. The man whom he most desired to meet in Italy was Garabaldi, for whom he had a sincere admiration; but it was not his fortune to see this veteran patriot. It was impossible, however, for the General to avoid the kind attentions which were shown him in Italy. At Rome, he was the recipient of many marked courtesies from King Humbert, who sent one of his own aides to conduct the General and his party through the city. The King also gave a magnificent banquet to General Grant, at which all the Italian Ministers were present. He was presented to the people by Cardinal McCloskey, then on a visit to Rome, and had a very agreeable interview with that distinguished prelate. At Florence the party met many Americans, and the General greatly enjoyed the visits to the galleries and museums of that home of art where so many treasures are collected. Pisa, with its famous Leaning Tower, was visited, and thence the party went to Venice, the "Queen of the Adriatic." Here the General greatly enjoyed the rides in the gondolas, which he thought far superior to street-cars or cabs—when the streets are, as at Venice, under water. Milan was the last Italian city visited, and here the General had an immense number of American callers and official visitors—not too many, however, to prevent him visiting the grand Duomo, with its pinnacles of pure white marble, surmounted by statues whose numbers are too great to be counted, and the wonderful and lovely frescoes which have made Milan famous in art.

At Palermo, in Sicily, General Grant declined the hospitalities of the town which were kindly proffered by the prefect who came to pay his respects to the General on board the "Vandalia," and went ashore with Captain Robeson, with whom he strolled for two or three hours about the place. Christmas was celebrated by a dinner given in honor of Mrs. Grant, by the officers of the "Vandalia," on board the vessel. In the evening there were fine displays of fireworks in the town and from the vessels in the harbor. Leaving Palermo, and passing Stromboli and Messina, and many other places of great historic interest, the "Vandalia" reached the famous island of Malta on the afternoon of December 28th. Here they found the British iron-clad "Sultan," whose commander, the Duke of Edinburgh, soon came on board the "Vandalia" to pay his respects to General Grant. His royal highness remained an hour in conversation with the General, who acknowledged the compliment of his visit by accepting an invitation to lunch

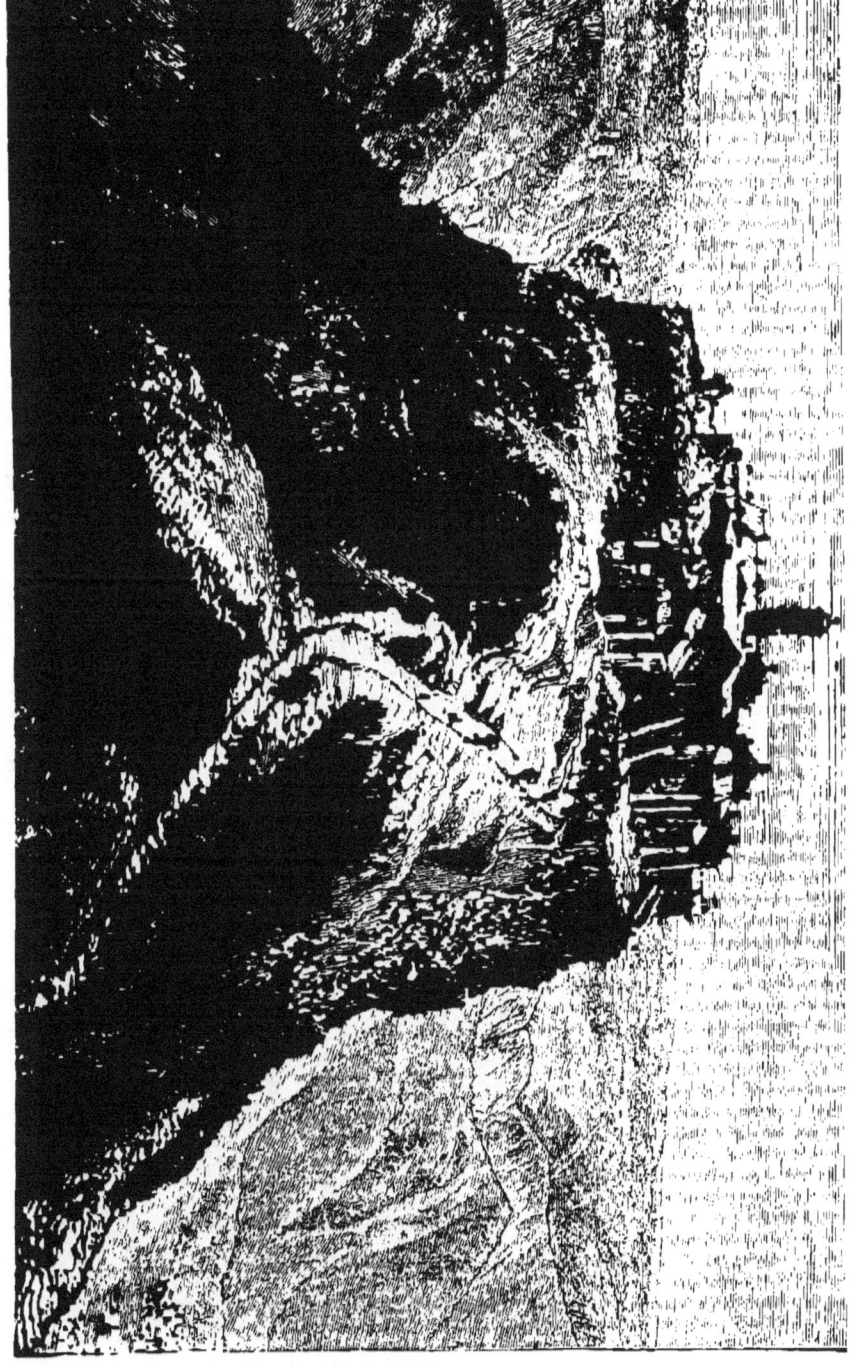

ITALY—CIVITA BAGNOREA.

ITALY.—ST. PETER AND THE VATICAN, FROM THE FALLS OF THE TIBER.

with the Duke at his palace at San Antonio. While at the Duke's palace General Grant received a visit from the Governor-General of Malta, with his council and a group of Maltese noblemen. Later in the day a state dinner was given to the General and party at the palace, and in the evening they all went to the opera, where the General was received with immense cheering, and the "Star Spangled Banner" was sung as he entered the theatre. The visit to Malta was a most enjoyable one, and the party left there with regret. On the last day of December, amid the music of the bands and the hearty cheers of the British sailors, the "Vandalia" left Malta and pushed her prow into the Mediterranean in the direction of Alexandria. The weather was cold and dismal, and the passage was marked by a fearful storm, which made the ship groan and stagger through the waves, and caused the water to pour in sheets into the cabin. But, as in the Atlantic voyage, the General showed himself an excellent sailor, and experienced but little discomfort—though most of the other passengers were in a sad state of sea-sick wretchedness. The next morning, however, the storm cleared away; and before the coast of Egypt was reached, the bright skies and genial sun of a delightful New Year's day had quite restored the cheerfulness of all on board the "Vandalia."

CHAPTER XI.

EGYPT AND THE NILE.

GRANT AND ALEXANDER — THE "VANDALIA" AT ALEXANDRIA—THE KHEDIVE'S HOSPITALITY— THE GENERAL AND STANLEY— THE GREAT MONOLETHS—AT CAIRO—UP THE NILE—MONUMENTS, RUINS AND TOMBS—UPPER EGYPT AND HER WONDERS, THEBES AND LYCOPOLIS—OFF FOR PALESTINE.

General Grant visited every continent, but the only portion of Africa which he explored was the land of the Pharaohs, and that he penetrated as far up the Nile as the first cataract. The original intention was to steer straight for Cairo, but the good anchorage of Alexandria was too tempting the party spent three days there. It was certainly eminently appropriate that General Grant should begin his African tour by a visit to the city founded by and named in honor of the greatest soldier of antiquity. He is himself the Alexander of the new world, and a good authority pronounces him the great soldier of the Saxon race, the race which produced a Marlborough and a Wellington. But he showed no disposition to link his name in any accidental way with that of the supreme warrior of Greece and conqueror of the world. In all his tastes and temper General Grant is preeminently pacific, as was frequently shown during his trip around the world. Nothing he said or did at Alexandria suggested any thought of the hero whose name that city perpetuates.

Hardly had the General's good ship, the "Vandalia," come to anchor before a distinguished party boarded her, intent on a cordial welcome to Egypt of the far more distinguished party about to land. The Governor of the district took the lead. With him came Beys, missionaries, Consul-General Farman and others. He extended formal welcome in the name of the Khedive, in whose behalf he offered a palace in Cairo; a special steamer for the trip up the Nile, and whatever else the ruler of Egypt could contribute to the pleasure of the visit. This was a foretaste of the Oriental honors which awaited the circumnavigator.

Before the day closed General Grant, accompanied by his son Jesse, and two or three officers, landed in the official barge. The "Vandalia" fired the official salute, twenty-one guns, which was returned by the Egyptain vessels in the harbor. A guard of honor added dignity to the occasion, and every thing was done in truly Oriental style. The Governor, or Pasha, was very gracious. He offered his guests cigarettes, and through an interpreter assured the General that Egypt was proud to see so illustrious a stranger. To this laconic address General Grant replied that he anticipated great pleasure in visiting Egypt. The conversation was anything but brisk. The great American sphinx, as he has often been called, was in the land of the sphinx, and the interview was largely devoted to pauses. Besides cigarettes the guests were offered in queer little cups cased in filigree mulled wine, mild but very hot. The call, with its hospitalities, conversation and pauses continued only a few moments, closing with solemn salaams after the fashion of the country. The episode was noticeable as the first experience of a kind of life in store for the traveler in his sun-rise journeyings.

That evening was spent in an Occidental rather then Oriental way. The consul, Mr. Salvage, had the General and his wife to dine with him. Besides the dinner there was a ball. The only notable feature of the evening was the presence of Henry M. Stanley. The two noted travelers were peculiarly companionable. There were no awkward pauses in their conversation. They sat and chatted cozily, the General taking a deep interest in the exploits of the great explorer. Very few Americans have traveled as far and seen as much as Grant, but neither he nor any other of our countrymen have penetrated the wilds of "the dark continent" as deeply as the plucky journalist who found Livingston and contributed so much to the knowledge of Africa. Toasts were proposed in honor of General Grant, Mrs. Grant and Stanley. The later had the grace to say that it was one of the proudest moments of his life to find himself seated by the side of the guest of the evening.

The next day, Sunday, was spent in quietly strolling about town. If any of the good missionaries who joined in greeting his advent preached that day, the recording angel of the party, better known as the *Herald* correspondent, made no note of any attendance upon the services. The General's time was precious. He was to leave the city the day following, and there were several interesting points to visit, a granite Monolith absurdly called Pompey's Pillar, the Catacombs two obelisks called Cleopatra's Needles, a magnificent harbor thoroughly modern, and the various peculiarities of a city curiously blending European enterprise with Oriental conservatism.

Four hours by rail and Cairo was reached. The Khedive delegated General Stone to bear his greeting to the guest. He is one of the "Confederate Brigadiers" who sought military service, after the war, in the land of the Pyramids. It seems that he was a fellow student with Grant at West Point. They had not met since their school-days. The General was very glad to see him. They talked of "Bonny Haven" days and seemed to enjoy it very much. The palace which had been assigned the General is known as Kassr-el. Doussa, and there the guest was made to feel quite at home. The jolly Sir John was not more at ease in "mine inn," than Grant in his palace.

At eleven o'clock the next morning the General called by appointment upon the Khedive, accompained by several naval officers, his son and Consul-General Farman. The party were conveyed thither in state carriages. The reception occupied about half an hour. Hardly had the General returned to his palace before the Khedive was announced, for in that respect, if in no other, the Orient is promptness itself. Dilatory in business but expeditious in etiquette seems to be the rule at the East.

Although the capital of modern Egypt, Cairo is not a city of much interest to travelers. It is situate on a sandy plain on the right bank of the Nile. Our traveler lost no time in availing himself of the facilities afforded him by the ruler of the country (since deposed) to go up the most wonderful and historically interesting river of all the world. Its navigation is intricate and difficult. Nature seems to have exhausted herself in trying to make it useful for enriching the Delta and making it productive, indifferent to its utility as a common carrier. But this steamer glided along as if there were no obstructions in the way. Guides, interpreters and scholars learned in the lore of the monuments and ruins to be visited, had been provided. The trip was delightful in every way. The first stopping place was Sioot, the capital of the province of the same name, a city of some 25,000 inhabitants. In ancient days the town was known as Lycopolis. It is the chief resort of the caravans from Nubia and Soodan. It is not on the river. The ride to it overland was through a country once rich in cereals, but now parched and sterile. As the party, under the escort of the American vice consul, a Syrian, approached the city, the people turned out to meet them, as if every man, woman and child were familiar with and delighted to honor the name of Grant. The *Herald's* representative, one of the party, writes: "All the town seemed to know of their coming, for wherever they went great crowds swarmed around, and they had to force their donkeys through masses of Arabs and Egyptians, of all ages and conditions. The stores are little holes of rooms, in front of which the trader sits and calls upon you to buy. As these avenues are less than six feet, one can imagine the trouble had in making progress. The town has some fine mosques and houses, but in the main is like all the towns of Upper Egypt, a collection of mud hovels. A grand reception was given by the Vice-Consul. The dinner was regal in its profusion and splendor, and consisted of fully twenty courses, all well served. When it was concluded, the son of the host arose, and, in remarkably clear and correct English, proposed the General's health. We give a fragment of this speech:

"Long have we heard and wondered," said the speaker, "at the strange progress which America has made during this past century by which she has taken the first position among the most widely civilized nations. She has so quickly improved in sciences, morals and arts that the world stands amazed at this extraordinary progress, which surpasses the swiftness of lightning. It is to the hard work of her great and wise men that all this advance is imputed, those who have shown to the world what wise, courageous, patriotic men can do. Let all the world look to America and follow her example—that nation which has taken as the basis of her laws and the object of her undertakings to maintain freedom and equality among her own people, and secure them for others, avoiding all ambitious schemes which would draw her into bloody and disastrous wars, and trying by all means to maintain peace internally and externally. The only two great wars upon which she has engaged were entered upon for pure and just purposes—the first for releasing herself from the English yoke and erecting her independence, and the other for stopping slavery and strength-

TODI.

TIVOLI.

Sketches in Italy.

NEAR THE SOURCE OF THE TIBER.

ORVIETO.

Sketches in Italy.

ening the union of the States; and well we know that it was mainly, under God, due to the talent, courage and wisdom of his excellency, General Grant, that the latter of the two enterprises was brought to a successful issue. The speech closed by a tribute to the General and the Khedive. General Grant said in response that nothing in his whole trip had so impressed him as this unexpected, this generous welcome in the heart of Egypt. He had anticipated great pleasure in his visit to Egypt, and the anticipation had been more than realized. He thanked his host, and especially the young man who had spoken of him with so high praise, for their reception. The dinner dissolved into coffee, conversation and cigars.

Four days after the party left Cairo we find them at Girgeh, one hundred and eight miles below Thebes and twelve miles from the ruins of Abydus, where stands the oldest Christian monastery in Egypt. From there, mounted on donkeys, the General and his friends set out for Abydus. The sun poured down his rays unrelentingly, if it was midwinter, but it would never do to neglect that most ancient of Egyptian cities. Here are the ruins of a temple of Osiris and a temple of Memnon, that Mecca of the ancient Egyptians. The burial place of kings and gods, even, (for it is a city of sacred tombs,) it is itself buried in sand, except as recent excavations have laid bare its hidden mysteries of death. The ancient Egyptians had an abiding faith in immortality and believed fully in the resurrection of the body. They paid more attention to the preservation of human dust than to the welfare of human beings. To see Abydus was to catch a glimpse of the superstition which built not only that city of the dead but those vast mausoleums, the pyramids. In so practical, sensible and thoroughly modern a man as Ulysses S. Grant, Egyptian ideas could hardly touch a single responsive chord.

The next point of interest was Thebes, Thebes of the hundred gates, with its palace of Luxor, temple of Kanark, statues of Memnon, and kindred marvels, the greatest of which is Kanark, or rather that series of temples to which it belongs, and which constitute the Thebes of to-day. The art of that far-away day and city was gigantic, sublime and vast, yet exquisite, with all, in its finish. Palaces and temples of the grandest character were connected by magnificent flights of steps and avenues of colossal sphinxes. The main hall of the Kanark is three hundred and twenty-nine feet long, one hundred and seventy-nine feet wide and eighty feet high. But we cannot stop to particularize. It may be added that the almost infinite contrast between the grandeur of the ancient monuments of superstition and the present squalid abodes of the few people who live beneath the shadows of those ruins eloquently protests against the folly of neglecting the actual for the imaginary. Even the Pasha of the province, who was all attention to General Grant, lived in a low brick building, more like a barrack than a palace.

A few other points of great but lesser interest were visited and then the steamer's prow was turned down stream, reaching Memphis, the successor and supplanter of Thebes, the third day of February. Then more tombs, temples and mausoleums were visited, including the serapeums of the sacred bulls. By this time visiting ruins had become somewhat monotonous, and all were glad to steam away in the morning down to Cairo. Three days were spent at the palace of Kassr-el-Doussa in taking needed rest, and then, like Moses and his fugitive slaves, the General and party were off for the land of Canaan, having spent a month in visiting Egypt and her sepulchral ruins up the Nile.

CHAPTER XII.

HOLY AND CLASSIC LANDS.

Sceptre of Universal Empire—From Port Saul to Jaffa—Joppa and the Crusades—"Welcome to Grant"—Off for Jerusalem—David and Goliah—Cavalry Escort—In the Holy City—Sacred Places—Suburbs of Jerusalem—Nazareth and Damascus—At Constantinople—Quiet Strolls—Through the Dardanelles—The Peræus Reached—King and Queen of Greece—Greek Art and Philosophy.

This chapter is almost wholly devoted to sight-seeing in the two lands which have made the deepest impression upon modern civilization of any countries of history, Palestine and Greece. The religion of the Hebrews and the art, poetry and philosophy of the Greeks may be said to share the sceptre of universal empires. It was not Rome that conquered the world with the sword, so much as Jerusalem with its sacred and Athens with its classic literature. General Grant is not a student of Biblical lore, nor a Gladstone in devotion to Homer and his literary children, being unable, probably, to read either Hebrew or Greek works in the original; but he was not content to go around the world without visiting the hive of the "Attic bee" and the "lands which floweth with milk and honey," or did, rather, for now it is "waster than a warren."

With his face set towards Zion, General Grant left Port Said in the "Vandalia," which had come thither from Alexandria to convey the ex-President from the land of father Nilus to the Land of Promise. No hurried crossing of the Red Sea and tedious delay in the wilderness was necessary in this case. A little smooth sailing and the change of countries was effected. Port Said was reached February 9th and Jaffa, or Joppa as it is best known to Bible readers, the day following.

It was Sunday, but not the Sabbath. That is a Mahommedan country, and Friday is the holy day of the week. The population of Jaffa is only five thousand, but it represents three of the four great religions of the world, the Mahommedan, the Christian, and the Hebrew. The Buddhists only are wanting to complete the list. Substantial freedom is enjoyed in the exercise of faith and the practice of worship. Jehovah, Jesus and Mahommed are worshipped, each in the way agreeable to the worshipper. Jaffa has three Sabbaths, although in our mode of observance it can hardly be said to have any at all.

Jaffa was the chief sea port of Canaan when the Hebrew theocracy was in its glory, which was just after it had been supplemented by the establishment of the monarchy. It was there that the material for Soloman's temple was landed on its way from Tyre to Jerusalem. It was there the Christians in the horrible days of the Crusade disbanded, and it was there, too, that the shattered hosts, or hordes of Peter the Hermit (the mediæval Moody) sought the sea as they recoiled from the scimetar of Islam and gave up in despair the insane idea of rescuing that hole in a rock known as the Holy Sepulchre, from Paynim profanation. It is only thirty-three miles from Jerusalem, in a northwestern direction.

Jaffa was not unmindful of the rank of its visitor. As he stepped ashore he passed under an arch way bearing in floral type, the inscription, " Welcome, to General Grant." The little town turned out en mass to testify the sincerity of the inscription. The vice consul, Hardegg, did what he could to make the party contented. But there was not much to see. The General was in Palestine to visit Jerusalem, and thither accompanied by his wife and several gentlemen, he wended his way without needless delay. Three ungainly wagons, each drawn by three horses, were procured for the journey. The first day brought them along the plain of Sharon, whose roses were not in bloom, as far as Ramleh where they halted for the night, but only to resume their journey at six in the morning. The fertility of the land, once so tempting to the ex-slaves in the wilderness, and which was so long the home of the most remarkable people in all history, has passed away. The route was dreary desolation, rough and sterile in the extreme. It was worse than riding over a corduroy road. As they reached their destination the travelers were compensated by the sight of several points of interest. The ruins of that once royal city, Gezer spread before them, but contemptible and mean were those remains, as compared with the grand ruins they had so recently left. Kirjath Jearim and the valley of Ajalon lay before them. The field whereon David met Goliah must have recalled memories of childhood, for few stories are more attractive in their suggestions than the tradition of how a mere stripling vanquished a giant in "the brave days of old." Many a boy has reflected, no doubt, upon the skill of the slinger whose aim was so fatally true with emulous admiration. The brook from which he picked his pebbles, babbled for General Grant as it had for that other Son of Jesse, chiliads, before.

Having crossed this ravine the quiet of the journey was over. A troop of cavalry started out from Jerusalem, to escort the world-famed traveler to the Sacred City. With the soldiers came representatives from all of the Consulates, delegations from the various nationalities represented in that city, Americans, Armenians, Jews, Greeks and others. The modest traveler found his entry not so very unlike that of Him who was hailed with hosannas as he came riding upon an ass. But there was no malicious priesthood to play upon the fears of Pilate and foment a popular reaction. The Pasha and the consuls made becoming haste to personally honor the General with a call. The patriarchs and clerical dignitaries of different faiths joined in honoring the visitor. A serenade by the Pashal band and a grand state dinner added to the pleasure of the occasion. It was only by early strolls that the General escaped from public demonstrations. He took up his abode while in the Holy City within a very short distance of that hotest of holy places, Calvary. His chamber window commanded a fine view of the Mount of Crucifixtion.

General Grant is not a particularly devout man, nor yet does he perplex himself with the doubts

CRETE.

CARTHAGE.

Sketches in the Holy Land

DELOS.

CUMÆ.

Sketches in the Holy Land.

of modern rationalism. In a common sense sort of way he accepts the faith of his childhood, Methodism. The places of interest in and about Jerusalem are, for the most part mythical, as regards the particular occurrences which they are claimed to have witnessed, and as such he regarded them. But even thus they possess a peculiar interest. The house for instance of the rich man of the parable is gravely pointed out, and the steps on which Lazarus reclined as he begged the crumbs which fell from the table of Dives. All these places the General visited, betraying no sign of incredulity. The identical spot where Jesus sank under the weight of the cross was pointed out to him with pious credence in its reality. An indented stone was pointed out to him as being the imprint of the sacred hand bearing for support beneath that cruel burden. The Via Dolorosia along which the Savior passed from the judgment hall to the place of execution is replete with evidences of amiable superstition. What impressions all these things made upon his mind must be left to conjecture, for the Sphinx listened, looked and pondered without comment.

Beyond the city lay the valley of Jehoshaphat, the brook Kedron and the Garden of Gethsemane with its "Tree of Agony" from which the priests gathered blossoms for Mrs. Grant. The

J

Mount of Olives is steep and high, but the General and his good wife pressed on to its summit, and briefly rested at the chapel, now a Moslem mosque, where Jesus is said to have ascended to his Father, his mediatorial work finished. From the minarets of that mosque they had a fine view of the Jordan, the Dead Sea and the Land of Moab. But the end was not yet. After a little repose the walk was resumed and the village of Bethany reached, where Lazarus and his two sisters kept what was probably an Essene inn, and to which Jesus loved to resort. Ruins and huts mark the spot hallowed by memories of a sacred friendship. Returning by another route they passed the supposed grave of Lazarus and along the road traversed by Jesus when he made his Messianic entry into Jerusalem, passing through the famous Damascus gate through which Saul of Tarsus passed as he went forth upon his errand of persecution, so soon to be changed into a missionary tour.

Having "done" Jerusalem and its suburbs quite thoroughly, General Grant departed as quietly as he could for Damascus, a city rich in biblical associations, stretching from Abraham to Paul, still not a part of the Holy Land.

The most interesting place visited between Jerusalem and Damascus was Nazareth, although Shiloh, Nain, Endor and Jenin had attractions of a historical nature; Nazareth having been the early home of Jesus, was peculiarily deserving the tribute of a visit. Nothing remains, however, to lift it above the level of mediocrity but its historical associations. It is reached by a steep descent and is embedded in the most fruitful plain of all Syria. The town is not wanting in spots of asserted interest, such as the dwelling of the Virgin Mary, all of which are absurdly mythical, and we hasten on to Damascus.

In the days when the Jews were a people with a country of their own, Damascus was the capital of Syria, a term which did not then, as now, include Palestine. In reaching that city General Grant passed through the plain held by the Arabs to be the fairest of the four earthly paradises, but it is sadly out of repair now. The Adams and Eves who inhabit it now are very poor gardeners. The city itself has some thrift, in spite of misrule, indolence and what a Yankee would call "shiftlessness." In that far-famed center of Syriac traffic one may form a very clear idea of oriental habits of mercantile business. But there was nothing to detain our traveler long. He soon bid adieu to the "City of Pleasure" and was off for Beyrout. That is an important town at the present time, but its historical associations do not extend farther back than the Crusades, and in that country "a thousand years is but as one day." To General Grant it mattered not that Baldwin captured it and Saladin wrested it from the Christians again. To him the place was little more than a point of embarkation.

Leaving the Holy Land and all the rest of Turkey in Asia behind him, the General was off for the Capital of Turkey, which he was to visit en route for the present Capital, as always the chief city of Greece.

General Grant's arrival at Constantinople was a few days after the treaty of San Stefano. The Turko-Russian war was over. It was the fifth day of March when the "Vandalia" reached Stamboul, where he was met by the diplomatic representatives of this country, and many of the Americans in Constantinople. The Turkish authorities were too much occupied to pay very much attention to the distinguished visitor. Had the Sultan landed at New York about the time the peace of Appomattox was negotiated, he would hardly have been noticed. General Grant liked this. He inspected the marvels of that marvelous city in a way quite to his taste. The British Ambassador, Sir Austin Henry Layard, did all in his power to honor the man who had received so much attention, especially in England. The weather was very disagreeable. The Black Sea seemed richly to deserve its name, and the

"Golden Horn" was lusterless. But the General was not to be daunted by fog and rain. There were mosques and other notable things to be seen, and he saw them. A member of the party wrote home that "Though the Russians were quite near, since peace had been declared business seemed to be reviving. Camels or the Turkish porters went briskly around, bent double under their heavy burdens, but were the only lively people on the scene. The Turkish merchant takes business in the most nonchalant way. He never is in a hurry. Prices we found were very exhorbitant, that is if we chose to pay them. The act of chaffering or haggling seems to be expected, and one's time and patience are sorely tried. It is not because you are an infidel or a stranger that ten times what a thing is worth is asked you, it is simply the habit of the country." And he might have added, the habit of the East, generally.

Having seen enough of Constantinople, the party once more betook themselves to the "Vandalia," and sailed through the Dardanelles into the gulf of Athens, to the port six miles distant from the renowned city of their destination, which was reached finally by rail.

General Grant confined his Grecian visit to Athens, except that he took a look at the immortal plain of Marathon, hard by. Historically speaking, Athens is only one of the many places of interest in that illustrious peninsula. The list is long, including Ithica, made illustrious by that earlier Ulysses, whose travels are also immortal. But for the purposes of ordinary travel to see Athens is to see Greece.

As General Grant's good ship, the "Vandalia," neared the port, which is none other than the illustrious harbor of Piræus, now called Drako, three Greek iron clads came out to gracefully escort her. A large crowd witnessed the landing. In due time the General and Mrs. Grant were presented to King George and Queen Olga, who did all they could to honor their guests. Banquets and luncheons were given, but the time was mainly occupied in sight-seeing. There was enough of that to fill out the week—the Acropolis, the Areopagus, better known as Mars Hill, and the Museum. Each had to be climbed, for each is rich in interest, especially the first and second. On the Acropolis still remains much of the Propylea, one of the master pieces of Athenean architecture, and better still, the Parthenon, the most perfect triumph of architectural genius the world ever produced. This marvelous structure remained almost entire until the seventeenth century, when the ravages of war made terrible havoc with its Phidian marbles. Other temples, hardly less grand and beautiful, exist in ruins,

ruins which tantalize the beholder by imperfect suggestions of a grandeur and stately beauty impossible in these days, which one is tempted to call degenerate. The Museum is the best preserved of all the monumental temples of Athens.

Besides inspecting the ruins of Athens proper, General Grant visited the grove, or academy, where Plato taught as a system the philosophy set forth in a rudimentary way by Socrates, also the lyceum over which Aristotle presided. Without being at all metaphysical in his taste, or making any pretentions to familiarity with classic literature, he having enjoyed the advantages of the thorough education West Point affords, found the trip to Athens replete with deep interest, and weighed anchor for Naples well pleased with the classic addenda to his travels in the Holy Land.

CHAPTER XIII.

HOLLAND.

Dutch Art—Two Weeks in Holland—A Triumph of Engineering Skill—At the Hague—To Rotterdam—Amsterdam, Formerly and Now—Banquet by the Merchants.

From classic Athens we go at one stride to matter of fact Holland. Between the two there could hardly be a sharper contrast, except that both can boast remarkable attainments in art. The plodding, painstaking Hollanders, Rubens, Paul Potter, Van Dyck, Ruysdael, Teniers and Gerard Douws, gave to the Dutch school of painting a rank second to none in the world. But our traveler did not go from one to the other without stopping by the way, although he could have done so. He followed, rather, the march of civilization, sailing first to Italy, bidding good

CONSTANTINOPLE—THE SULTAN'S PALACE ON THE BOSPHORUS.

TURKISH LADY.

OBELISK OF THEODOSIUS.
Sketches in Constantinople.

bye forever to the "Vandalia" in the beautiful Bay of Naples. Thence he went by easy stages to Paris by rail, stopping to visit Rome and several other points of interest. At Paris he remained until the warm weather drove him northward. What he saw and how he was treated in Italy and Paris has been told already. It is enough to add here that he left the "City of Luxuries," as the latest, and we hope the last Napolean was fond of calling his capital, when all around him and on the way suggested Lowell's exclamation: "What is so rare as a day in June!"

The Dutch cities visited by General Grant were, naming them in the order of their visitation, the Hague, or Gravenhagen, as the Court Capital is called at home; Rotterdam; Amsterdam; Brœk; Haarlem and Hanover. The time spent in the country was a fortnight. Everywhere nature presented the same aspect. The views soon became stale, for the land *is* flat, but very profitable, withal. The fields were as green as a prairie in June, and the cattle somewhat sleeker than the kine of this country. One can not fully appreciate Paul Potter's art without seeing the bulls of Holland. General Grant, however, was more interested in the engineering genius which had rescued that country from the waves than he was in art or husbandry. His West Point

Amsterdam is the larger of the two, having a population of about 300,000. It is the Constitutional Capital of Holland, as the Hague is its Court Capital. Once it was the chief commercial city of the world, and not very long ago, either. The period of its greatness was from 1630 to 1750. Gallant and almost supernatural, (using the term in a strictly material sense) effort was made to reclaim that supremacy; but nature was exceedingly forward. The filling up of the Zuyder Zee and the Pamprus Bar placed obstructions in the way of navigation that the most wonderful engineering could not obviate, and Amsterdam had to accept the situation. General Grant found the inspection of its canals, wharfs and dykes none the less interesting, however, on that account. Holland abounds in canals, but it is at Amsterdam that the Dutch system of canalage is seen to best advantage. It cuts up the city into some ninety islands, rendering necessary two hundred and eighty-five bridges.

Amsterdam is in some respects like Chicago. In both cities if the writer were to go to only one place, that place should be on 'Change. While only the products of prairie farms are bought and sold on the Chicago Board of Trade, the merchants of Amsterdam meet daily at their great mart to buy and sell produce and wares from all parts of the world. It was with great propriety that the banquet given to General Grant in that city came from the merchants. Some fifty of the merchant princes joined in giving it, and all the dignitaries of the city were in attendance. The Hollanders have always been very friendly to this country, and they took a great liking to the General, his quiet ways and fondness for a cigar commending him to their especial good graces. And after the whirl and unrest of Paris the repose of the Netherlands was peculiarly agreeable.

Mention has been made of Brœk and Haarlem. Both may be said to be suburbs of Amsterdam. The former is noted for its neatness and the latter for having the grand organ of the world, that in the church of St. Bavon. The organist took pleasure in playing it to the best possible advantage for the General.

It may be added that on the way to Berlin, whither the party went from Amsterdam, a brief visit was paid to Hanover, the cradle of British royalty. The Palace of the Harrenhausen is interesting, and the Hanoverian stables which have so long furnished the horses for the use of royalty on state occasions in England, had some attractions for our *equiphilious* Ex-President.

CHAPTER XIV.

BERLIN AND BISMARCK.

The Visit to the German Capital—Attempted Assassination of the Emperor—General Grant and the International Peace Congress—The Meeting with Prince Bismarck—A Remarkable Interview Between two Remarkable Men—Their Views of Persons and Things—General Grant and Bayard Taylor.

It was during the General's brief sojourn in Holland that the German Emperor was shot and seriously, but not fatally, wounded. That was one of a series of futile attempts at regicide during that year, one of which General Grant was destined to see the next winter during his visit at Madrid. The visit to the German Capital was delayed a little on that account, and modified a good deal. The imperial honors which would undoubtedly have been shown him, were mainly omitted. Every demonstration of respect was tempered and subdued like footsteps in a sick room.

Without dwelling at all upon the peculiarities of Berlin, which, with all its greatness, is not very interesting, this chapter will be devoted almost wholly to the feature of General Grant's visit which stands conspicuous, namely: his interview with Bismarck. The Congress of Nations, then in session at Berlin for the settlement of the questions connected with the Turko-Russian war, especially interested General Grant, for it was a test of arbitration as a substitute for war, and as President of the United States he was the especial promoter of arbitration. But with the Congress he had nothing to do.

Arriving at Berlin, June 26th, under the escort of the late lamented Bayard Taylor, then the American Minister at the German Court, he lost very little time in making himself acquainted with all parts of the city.

Speaking of the International Peace Congress as a feature of General Grant's tour, the New York *Herald* correspondent wrote:

"All distinguished diplomats seem to be gouty, and as Prince Gortschakoff was afflicted with this aristocratic disease, at the request of the Russian Plenipotentiary, General Grant called on the Prince. It was Mr. Bayard Taylor who arranged the visit. Prince Gortschakoff was highly pleased with the compliment paid to his country. Of all the members of the great European Congress, now holding their session in Berlin, most of the foreign representatives, Lord Beaconsfield, Lord Salisbury, M. Waddington, and Count Corti were known to the General. Mehemet Ali the General had met in Turkey. Visits of ceremony had to be paid to all these dignitaries. Among the very first of the great ones of this earth who left his card for the Ex-President was Prince Bismarck. Unfortunately General Grant was absent, and the visit on the part of Bismarck was repeated. As the General was most anxious to make the acquaintance of the great German, for whose character and services he had so high an admiration, the calls were returned at once, and a message was sent his highness, saying that the General would call at any time which would suit his convenience."

Although Bismarck's relations to that Congress made him its central figure, the interview referred to was quite independent of that Congress, and was the natural result of the meeting of the most remarkable public men of their day. Omitting some of the non-essentials, we give the interview as reported by the correspondent referred to:

Prince Bismarck wears an officer's uniform, and as he takes the General's hand, he says, "Glad to welcome General Grant to Germany."

The General's reply is "that there is no incident in his German tour more interesting to him than this opportunity of meeting the Prince." Prince Bismarck then expressed surprise at finding the General so young a man; but when a comparison of ages is made, Prince Bismarck finds that the Ex-President is only eleven years his junior.

THE RHINE—MERCHANTS' EXCHANGE, AT CONSTANCE.

THE RHINE—JUVALTA.

"That," says the prince, "shows the value of a military life, for here you have the frame of a young man, while I feel like an old one."

The General smiled, observing that he was at that period of life when he could have no higher compliment paid him than that of being called a young man. By the time this pleasant chatting had been going on, the prince had offered the General a seat. All this took place in a library or study. There was an open window which looked out on the beautiful park on which the June sun was shining. This was the private park of the Radziwill Palace, which is now Bismarck's Berlin home. The library was a large, spacious room, the walls of gray marble, and the furniture plain and simple. In one corner stood a large, high writing-desk, where the Chancellor works, and on the waxed floor a few Turkish rugs were thrown. The prince speaks English with precision, though slowly from want of practice, and when he wants a word seeks refuge in French. He shows however, that he has a fair command of our venacular.

One of the prince's first questions was about General Sheridan.

"The General and I," said the prince, "were fellow campaigners in France, and we became great friends."

General Grant said that he had had letters from Sheridan recently and he was quite well.

"Sheridan," said the prince, "seemed to be a man of great ability."

"Yes," answered the General, "I regard Sheridan as not only one of the great soldiers of our war, but one of the great soldiers of the world—as a man who is fit for the highest commands. No better general ever lived than Sheridan."

"I observed," said the prince, "that he had a wonderfully quick eye. On one occasion, I remember, the Em-

K

peror and his staff took up a position to observe a battle. The Emperor himself was never near enough to the front; was always impatient to be as near the fighting as possible. "Well,' said Sheridan to me, as we rode along, 'we shall never stay here, the enemy will in a short time make this so untenable that we shall all be leaving in a hurry. Then while the men are advancing they will see us retreating.' Sure enough, in an hour or so the cannon shot began to plunge this way and that way, and we saw we must leave. It was difficult to move the Emperor, however; but we all had to go, and," said the prince, with a hearty laugh, "we went rapidly. Sheridan had seen it from the beginning. I wish I had so quick an eye."

The prince then asked about Sheridan's command—his exact rank, his age, how long he held the command, and remarked that he was about the same age as the Crown Prince.

The General made a reference to the deliberations of the Congress, and hoped that there would be a peaceful result.

"That is my hope and belief," said the prince. "That is all our interest in the matter. We have no business with the Congress whatever, and are attending to the business of others by calling a Congress. But Germany wants peace, and Europe wants peace, and all our labors are to that end. In the settlement of the question arising out of the San Stefano Treaty, Germany has no interest of a selfish character. I suppose," said the prince, "the whole situation may be summed up in this phrase: in making the treaty, Russia ate more than she could digest, and the main business of the Congress is to relieve her. The war has been severe upon Russia, and of course she wants peace."

The General asked how long the Congress would probably sit, and the prince answered that he thought seven or eight more sittings would close the business. "I wish it were over, he said, "for Berlin is warm and I want to leave it."

The prince said, that another reason why he was sorry the Congress was in session was that he could not take General Grant around and show him Berlin. He said also that the Emperor himself was disappointed in not being able to see the General.

"His majesty," said the prince, "has been expecting you, and evinces the greatest interest in your achievements, in the distinguished part you have played in the history of your country, and in your visit to Germany. He commands me to say that nothing but his doctor's orders that he shall see no one, prevents his seeing you."

The General said, "I am sorry that I cannot have that honor, but I am far more sorry for the cause, and hope the Emperor is recovering."

"All the indications are of the best," answered the prince. "for the Emperor has a fine constitution and great courage and endurance, but you know he is a very old man."

"That," said the General, "adds to the horror one feels for the crime."

"It is so strange, so strange and so sad," answered the prince, with marked feeling. Here is an old man—one of the kindest old gentlemen in the world—and yet they must try and shoot him! There never was a more simple, more genuine, more—what shall I say—more humane character than the Emperor's. He is totally unlike men born in his station, or many of them at least. You know that men who come into the world in his rank, born princes, are apt to think themselves of another race and another world. They are apt to take small account of the wishes and feelings of others. All their education tends to deaden the human side. But this Emperor is so much of a man in all things! He never did any one a wrong in his life. He never wounded any one's feelings; never imposed a hardship! He is the most genial and winning of men—thinking always, anxious always for the comfort and welfare of his people—of those around him. You cannot conceive a finer type of the noble, courteous, charitable old gentleman, with every high quality of a prince, as well as every virtue of a man. I should have supposed that the Emperor could have walked alone all over the Empire without harm, and yet they must try and shoot him."

The General said that it was a horrible thing, and referred to Lincoln—a man of the kindest and gentlest nature—killed by an assassin.

"In some respects," said the prince, continuing as if in half a reverie, and as if speaking of a subject upon which he had been thinking a great deal—"In some respects the Emperor resembles his ancestor, Frederick William, the father of Frederick the Great. The difference between the two is that the old king would be severe and harsh at times to those around him, while the Emperor is never harsh to any one. But the old king had so much simplicity of character, lived an austere, home-loving, domestic life; had all the republican qualities. So with this king; he is so republican in all things that even the most extreme republican if he did his character justice would admire him."

The General answered that the influence which aimed at the Emperor's life was an influence that would destroy all government, all order, all society, republics and empires.

"In America," said General Grant, "some of our people are, as I see from the papers, anxious about it. There is only one way to deal with it, and that is by the severest methods. I don't see why a man who commits a crime like this, a crime that not only aims at an old man's life, a ruler's life, but shocks the world, should not meet with the severest punishment. In fact," continued the General, "although at home there is a strong sentiment against the death penalty, and it is a sentiment which one naturally respects, I am not sure but it should be made more severe rather than less severe. Something is due to the offended as well as the offender, especially where the offended is slain."

"That," said the prince, "is entirely my view. My convictions are so strong that I resigned the government of Alsace because I was required to commute sentences of capital nature. I could not do it in justice to my conscience. You see, this kind old gentleman, that Emperor whom these very people have tried to kill, is so gentle that he will never confirm a death sentence. Can you think of anything so strange that a sovereign whose tenderness of heart has practically abolished the death punishment should be the victim of assassination, or attempted assassination? That is the fact. Well, I have never agreed with the Emperor on this point, and in Alsace, when I found that as Chancellor I had to approve all commutations of the death sentence, I resigned. In Prussia that is the work of the Minister of Justice; in Alsace it devolved upon me. I felt as the French say, that something was due to justice, and if crimes like these are rampant they must be severely punished."

"All you can do with such people," said the General quietly, "is to kill them."

"Precisely so," answered the prince.

Prince Bismarck said the Emperor was especially sorry that he could not in person show General Grant a review, and that the Crown Prince would give him one. "But," said the prince, "the old gentleman is so much of a soldier and so fond of his army that nothing would give him more pleasure than to display it to so great a soldier as yourself."

The General said that he had accepted the Crown Prince's invitation to a review for next morning, but with a smile continued: "The truth is I am more of a farmer than a soldier. I take little or no interest in military affairs, and although I entered the army thirty-five years ago and have been in two wars, in Mexico as a young lieutenant, and later, I never went into the army without regret and never retired without pleasure."

"You are so happily placed," replied the prince, "in America that you need fear no wars. What always seemed so sad to me about your last great war was that you were fighting your own people. That is always so terrible in wars, so very hard."

"But it had to be done," said the General.

"Yes," said the prince, "you had to save the Union just as we had to save Germany."

"Not only save the Union, but destroy slavery," answered the General.

"I suppose, however, the Union was the real sentiment, the dominant sentiment," said the prince.

"In the beginning, yes," said the General; "but as soon as slavery fired upon the flag it was felt, we all felt, even those who did not object to slaves, that slavery must be destroyed. We felt that it was a stain to the Union that men should be bought and sold like cattle."

"I had an old and good friend, an American, in Motley," said the Prince, "who used to write me now and then. Well, when your war broke out he wrote me. He said, 'I will make a prophecy, and please take this letter and put it in a tree or a box for ten years, then open it and see if I am not a prophet. I prophesy that when this war ends the Union will be established and we shall not lose a village or a hamlet.' This was Motley's prophecy," said the prince, with a smile, "and it was true."

"Yes," said the General, "it was true."

"I suppose if you had had a large army at the beginning of the war it would have ended in a much shorter time."

"We might have had no war at all," said the General; "but we cannot tell. Our war had many strange features—there were many things which seemed odd enough at the time, but which now seem Providential. If we had had a large regular army, as it was then constituted, it might have gone with the South. In fact, the Southern feeling in the army among high officers was so strong that when the war broke out the army dissolved. We had no army—then we had to organize one. A great commander like Sherman or Sheridan even then might have organized an army and put down the rebellion in six months or a year, or at the farthest, two years. But that would have saved slavery, perhaps, and slavery meant the germs of a new rebellion. There had to be an end of slavery. Then we were fighting an enemy with whom we could not make a peace. We had to destroy him. No convention, no treaty was possible—only destruction."

"It was a long war," said the prince, "and a great work well done—and I suppose it means a long peace."

"I believe so," said the General.

The prince asked the General when he might have the pleasure of seeing Mrs. Grant. The General answered that she would receive him at any convenient hour.

"Then," said the prince, "I will come to-morrow before the Congress meets."

Both gentlemen arose, and the General renewed the expression of his pleasure at having seen a man who was so well known and so highly esteemed in America.

"General," answered the prince, "the pleasure and the honor are mine. Germany and America have always been in such friendly relationship that nothing delights us more than to meet Americans, and especially an American who has done so much for his country, and whose name is so much honored in Germany as your own."

The prince and the General walked side by side to the door, and after shaking hands the General passed into the square. The guard presented arms, the General lit a fresh cigar, and slowly strolled home.

"I am glad I have seen Bismarck," the General remarked. "He is a man whose manner and bearing fully justify the opinions one forms of him. What he says about the Emperor was beautifully said, and should be known to all the Germans and those who esteem Germany."

Notable among incidents of the Berlin stay was a quiet informal reception given to the General by Mr. Bayard Taylor, our American Minister. Mr. Taylor was not aware of the General's coming until a day or two before his arrival, and had been quite ill. Then he had had no personal acquaintance with the General, and if his home political sympathies ran in one direction more than in another it was not in the direction of the General. But the two men became fast friends. They met several times afterward, once at a grand dinner given in the General's honor by the Prince, but, their other conversations were merely the exchange of courtesies. Minister Taylor gave a banquet also, which was a very superb affair.

The General witnessed a military review and sham battle on a large scale. The Crown Prince and Princess did what they could to honor the General and Mrs. Grant. The time allowed for Berlin was short, but the warm weather urged our party northward, and July 2, Hamburg was reached, *en route* for Copenhagen and the Norseland in general.

CHAPTER XV.

THE NORSE COUNTRIES.

GENERAL GRANT IN HAMBURG—A FOURTH OF JULY CELEBRATION—THE GENERAL'S SPEECH—OFF FOR NORSELAND—TRAVELS IN DENMARK, NORWAY AND SWEDEN—A CORDIAL WELCOME FROM THE SKANDINAVIANS—A RIDE IN A NORWEGIAN "GO-CART"—CURIOSITIES OF STOCKHOLM.

General Grant was in Hamburg Independence day. There was special propriety in that. It is one of the old Hanseatic Confederation, a free city, governed by a Senate and a burgomaster. Nominally a part of the present German Empire, it is really a municipal republic. Every possible honor was shown the General by the Hamburgers. A dinner on the Fourth was given by the Vice Consul, participated in by about thirty Americans of both sexes. The chief toast of the occasion was "The man who had saved the country." The General responded as follows:

"MR. CONSUL AND FRIENDS: I am much obliged to you for the kind manner in which you drink my health. I share with you in all the pleasure and gratitude which Americans so far from home should feel on this anniversary. But I must dissent from one remark of our consul, to the effect that I saved the country during the recent war. If our country could be saved or ruined by the efforts of any one man, we should not have a country, and we should not be now celebrating our Fourth of July. There are many men who would have done far better than I did under the circumstances in which I found myself during the war. If I had never held command; if I had fallen; if all our Generals had fallen, there were ten thousand behind us who would have done our work just as well, who would have followed the contest to the end and never surrendered the Union. Therefore it is a mistake and a reflection upon the people to attribute to me, or to any number of us who held high commands, the salvation of the Union. We did our work as well as we could, and so did hundreds of thousands of others. We deserve no credit for it, for we should have been unworthy of our country and of the American name if we had not made every sacrifice to save the Union. What saved the Union was the coming forward of the young men of the nation. They came from their homes and fields, as they did in the time of the Revolution, giving everything to the country. To their devotion we owe the salvation of the Union. The humblest soldier who carried a musket is entitled to as much credit for the results of the war as those who were in command. So long as our young men are animated by this spirit there will be no fear for the Union."

Two days later the General was on the way once more, passing through Schleswig-Holstein and a part of Denmark, finding rest first at Copenhagen, the capital of Denmark. It is quite a modern city, gay, enterprising and prosperous. The country of which it is the capital is not under very fine cultivation. The people are much better than the soil, and the water is more profitable than the land. General Grant was pressed to make a somewhat extended tour of Denmark, the people and the authorities showing great zeal in his honor; but he tarried only to see the principal sights of the capital. The Rosenberg, "Castle of Roses;" the Metropolitan Church, "the True Kirk;" the University, and the Museums of Northern Antiquities and of Thorwaldsen, were visited. They tell the story of two Denmarks, the one belonging to the old days when the Dane bore sway over the Baltic from the vantage ground of occupying the entrance to it, the other belongs to a very modern Rennessaince. Hamlet is a tradition of the former, the art of Thorwaldsen and the romances of Hans Anderson are the glory of the latter.

Going northward through the Cattegat and along the south-west coast of Sweden, the General reached Gottenburg, a city of about sixty thousand inhabitants. A cordial welcome was extended to him. And it may be said right here that wherever he went in either Sweden or Norway, the people all along the line of travel turned out to greet him as if he were the National hero, their own Ulysses, back again from long wanderings in far lands. The truth is that there are so many Scandinavians in the United States that his name had become familiar to their friends at home. Throughout the Northwest they are scattered. During the war they were intensely patriotic, and always have been identified, with hardly an exception, with the same political party as General Grant. Year after year his fame in the far north had been spread by adopted American citizens. All classes joined everywhere in the manifestations of honor. The humble fishermen left their nets to swell the volume of popular enthusiasm, and when the General reached Christiana from Gottenburg he found that King Oscar had hastened home from a long distance to pay fitting honor to his more than regal guest. Every village passed joined in the tribute of respect. At Christiana no less than ten thousand people thronged the quay, nearly one-sixth of the entire population.

There was nothing very remarkable to be seen there, only the scenery is specially grand. The fjord of the same name is a magnificent stretch of water. Hills and headlands give grandeur to the view.

The most interesting feature of this Norse trip was an excursion in which the traveling was by "karjolers" and "stolkjærrers." Mr. John Russell Young, who was the literary member of the party, thus describes these modes of travel:

"Though the best turnouts had been provided for us, still they were of a peculiar rattle-trap appearance. The karjoler may be described as a low gig, a kind of clumsy sulky, holding one person; it has shafts made of good elastic wood, and the weight of the traveler is supported on the axletree and the horse's neck. I call it a horse through courtesy, though it is a pony, and a very small one at that. Your luggage, which must not be large (a Saratoga trunk would be an impossibility), is lashed on a frame on the axletree, and perched on that, clinging there for dear life, is a small boy, or sometimes a white-haired, blue-eyed little girl. This appendage does not pretend to drive you, but has the whole concern in his or her safe keeping. Having thus described the Norwegian go-cart, I have to say that with the exception of the American buggy, it is the most comfortable of all vehicles. It must have been invented for the peculiarities of the country. In any other kind of a drag it would have been impossible to scale the high, rough, rocky hillsides, or to go down into the valleys. It is delightful to exercise one's Jehulike propensities, and to guide the willing little steeds. These sturdy little brutes were as tractable as possible, good-tempered, intelligent, and ambitious. Perhaps the choice ponies of Norway had been selected for us. Now as to the other conveyance, the stolkjærrer, or seat-cart. Some of the party (for we had been joined by a number of American friends who had come a long way out of their road to pay their respects to the General) decided to try the seat-cart. I do not think they will ever make another essay of that character. They declared that after the first mile they expected to be shaken into fragments. Means of travel by these simple carriages are, of course, necessary in Norway; perhaps journeys could not be undertaken in any other way. In winter, railroads in certain districts would be difficult to manage, and then again the business would be limited.

This excursion over, the General was pressed to go fishing, but he has no more taste for that than for hunting. After accepting and returning the courtesies of the King he took the cars for Stockholm by Kingsvinger. The ride was over a country more picturesque than fertile. On his arrival he received an invitation to visit the Palace of Drottningholm, the grandest of the gay residences of Swedish royalty. "I think" writes Mr. Young, "the Ex-President, though he has seen innumerable palaces, would rather go from the garret of a regal residence to the cellar than see a review. Somehow I fancy the King half suspects this, and military pageants, save of a very mild character, do not interfere with the General's pleasures."

Stockholm is a city of nearly two hundred thousand inhabitants, "beautiful for situation," as seen in midsummer, being located at the outlet of Lake Malar into the Baltic. It dates back to Birger Jarl in the fourteenth century. Its palaces, museums, factories and libraries are imposing, but its church architecture is not at all imposing.

Several very grand masterpieces of memorial art, stone and bronze, have been erected. The founder of the city and several other public men of renown are thus honored, including Gustavus IV. It did not take General Grant long to see all that he cared to see at Stockholm, and he was soon off for Russia, across the Baltic.

CHAPTER XVI.

RUSSIA AND POLAND.

Across the Baltic—A Visit to the Northern Bear—Honors at Cronstadt—Arrival at St. Petersburg—Reception by the Emperor Alexander—His Familiarity with American Affairs—Chats with Gortschakoff and the Grand Duke Alexis—A Matter of Diplomacy—Why General Grant did not Visit the Russian Headquarters While in Turkey—Display by the St. Petersburg Fire Brigade—A "Buggy Ride" in Russia—Excursion Down the Harbor—Off for Moscow—Poland and its Sorrows.

Leaving Stockholm the latter part of July, General Grant and party made the voyage to St. Petersburg by steamship across the Baltic and through the great Gulf of Finland. The distance is nearly five hundred miles—one of the longest sea voyages made by the party since crossing the Atlantic. But they are good travelers by this time, both on land and sea; and they are but little disturbed by this long Baltic voyage, even by the rough northern gale which they encounter off the coast of Finland. At the head of the Gulf of Finland, is the Russian seaport of Cronstadt, where the party tarried for only a few hours, but still long enough to note that the vessels in the harbor are gay with flags displayed in the General's honor, while the guns from the shore batteries and the great ships of war greet him with a deafening salute. Even Russia, the most cold-blooded and stolid of nations, is not insensible to the presence of the illustrious American visitor, and the usual formalities of passports are dispensed with in his case. After a brief address of welcome from the authorities at Cronstadt—which must have greatly impressed the General, for he said nothing to the contrary —the party were transferred to another vessel, and, soon entering the Neva river, continued the journey to the Russian Capital.

Immediately on arriving at St. Petersburg (July 30th), the American Minister, Mr. Stoughton, called to pay his respects to General Grant; and he was followed by Prince Gortschakoff and other high officers of the Imperial Court. The next day the General was presented to the

Emperor Alexander, who received him with the utmost cordiality. A long and highly interesting conversation followed, mainly on American affairs, and especially on our relations with the Indian tribes, with which matters the Emperor showed surprising familiarity. Prince Gortschakoff, also, seemed desirous of conversing on American affairs, and made a most favorable impression upon the General's mind by his mild and winning manner no less than his profundity and originality of thought. A very agreeable conversation was had with the Grand Duke Alexis, who recalled many pleasant incidents of his visit to America some years ago, and made numerous inquiries of the General regarding people with whom he became acquainted in this country. He expressed much grief over the death of General Custer, whom he knew here, and for whose character he entertained the highest admiration.

It is worth noting here that at the time of General Grant's visit to Turkey, during the Russian occupation of Stefano, he was anxious to visit the Russian head-quarters, but decided not to do so, as he thought that, having been the guest of the Sultan, who had shown him great kindness and attention, it would be ungracious for him to go from the palace of his host to the head-quarters of a conquering army encamped in the suburbs of the Capital. There was some criticism at the time, some censure of General Grant for what was an apparent discourtesy in not visiting the Russian army; but it is now known that the General decided not to go out of consideration for the feelings of his host. He preferred to see the Russians in Russia. The General's sense of delicacy and propriety was undoubtedly correct; and that it was fully understood and appreciated by Russia, is evident from his cordial treatment while in that country. He received the most direct and flattering attentions from the leading officers of the army, as well as from the highest nobility and from the Emperor. The latter, at the close of General Grant's interview, accompanied him to the door, expressing the most friendly sentiments and saying, "Since the foundation of your government, relations between Russia and America have been of the friendliest character, and as long as I live nothing shall be spared to continue this friendship." The General's reply was to the effect that although the two Governments were very opposite in their character, the great majority of the American people were in sympathy with Russia, which good feeling he hoped would long continue.

While at St. Petersburg General Grant had an opportunity to witness a display of the city fire brigade, which greatly interested him. There were many rides about the city to see the wonderful sights, in droskies and other odd-looking Russian vehicles. The tarantass, which is the national carriage, is very peculiar in appearance. It has no springs, it is four-wheeled, and is sometimes like a wagon or phaeton. To it are harnessed three horses, all abreast. The middle beast is in the shafts, while the outside horses are hooked on by splinter bars. Russians are generally particular as to colors in horses; a bay or a roan takes the shafts, while the outsiders are black or dun. The middle horse trots, while his mates gallop. There is a high yoke over the horse in shafts, and to this a bell or series of bells is suspended, though sometimes both outside horses have collars with small bells. There is something exceedingly exhilerating in going at the full jump behind the three horses, one at a good trot, and the others at a rapid gallop. As General Grant is known to be very fond of riding, it is hardly necessary to add that all this was very novel and pleasing to him.

An excursion was made by water down the harbor to Peterhoff, a magnificent city, and as far as Cronstadt, at the mouth of the Neva river, in an imperial yacht which had been placed at the General's disposal by the Russian Government. On this excursion a visit was paid to the great Russian man-of-war. "Peter the Great," which fired a salute of twenty-one guns in the General's honor. The harbor was crowded with ships of war and other vessels, which displayed the American flag, while from their bands was heard the well-beloved national airs of America. Everything, in fact, connected with General Grant's reception at St. Petersburg was on a scale of regal magnificence, and he left them deeply impressed with the friendship felt for him and his country, as well as with the power and splendor of the Russian Empire.

From St. Petersburg, the new Capital of Russia, to Moscow, the old Capital, is a distance of four hundred miles, nearly in an air line. General Grant found the railroad between these two points equipped and managed in the American style, an elegant special carriage being placed at his disposal for the journey. The country traversed is dreary and monotonous, and the party were all glad when they reached Moscow. A large crowd were in waiting to receive them at the station, among whom were many Russian officers of high rank, and a number of Americans. Moscow is one of the most unique and famous cities in the world, and the few days devoted by General Grant to seeing its sights were full of interest and pleasure.

From Moscow, the party proceeded by rail to the equally famous Polish city of Warsaw, a distance of six hundred miles. Poland is the most unfortunate and pathetic country in the world. Its people are high-minded and chivalrous, but for more than a century have been ground down in hopeless servitude by their Russian masters. They are ruled by an iron and despotic hand. Even their own language is prohibited, the children being compelled to learn in school the language of their hated Russian conquerors. There is but little in this melancholy country to interest or divert the traveler; its settled sadness and hopelessness are painful and depressing; and after a few days at Warsaw, General Grant was glad to leave the gloomy old city—taking with him, however, a new sense of pride in his own free and happy country, and of patriotic gratitude for the privileges of liberty enjoyed so fully by all Americans.

CHAPTER XVII.

AUSTRIA, BAVARIA, AND THE VINEYARD OF FRANCE.

Arrival at Vienna—Meeting with Count Andrassy—Reception by the Emperor—Visit to the Imperial Arsenal—Munich and its Art—In France—Lyons and St. Etienne—Among the French Vineyards—A Picturesque Scene—Bordeaux and its Products.

Crossing the Austrian frontier from Poland, the city of Vienna was reached by General Grant on the 18th of August. Here he was met by the American Minister, Mr. Kasson, and the other members of the American Legation, and by many of his fellow-citizens stopping in Vienna. On the next day the General met the great Austrian Chancellor, Count Andrassy, and other eminent statesmen, at the rooms of the

AUSTRIA—THE ROSENGARTEN, FROM BOTZEN.

AUSTRIA—MONTE ANTELAO.

American Legation; and in the evening he dined at Count Andrassy's residence. The following day General Grant was received by the Emperor Francis Joseph, at the Imperial Palace of Schoenbrunn. On the 21st the General was taken to the Arsenal, where he was greatly interested in noting the improvements made in the Austrian artillery. A dinner with the Imperial family, a grand diplomatic banquet given by the American Minister, and a magnificent reception and ball, attended by the leading diplomats and most distinguished people in Vienna, were among the most prominent incidents of the General's stay in the gay Austrian capital.

From Vienna, General Grant's objective point was Spain, he having received a most cordial invitation from the King of that country to honor him with a visit. The route thither lay through Bavaria and Switzerland, and thence through the famous wine countries of Southern France. In passing through Bavaria, the party made a brief stop at Munich, famous alike for its art and beer; then to the antique city of Augsburg, where Luther drew up his Protestant declaration of faith; and at Ulm, on the bank of the Danube. From thence, a rapid ride through Switzerland took them to the French frontier, and they soon reached Lyons, the great silk manufacturing city of France. Only a brief stay was made here, as also at St. Etienne, another great manufacturing town, celebrated for its cutlery and for the manufacture of arms for the French service. Leaving these towns behind, the party were soon among the pleasant hillsides and vineyards of Normandy, famous wherever good wine is known. It was in the height of the grape-picking season; and all were delighted with the picturesque and animated scene, as the women and children, in their gay peasant attire, clipped the heavy bunches, which the men gathered in baskets and carried on their backs to the wine-press, from which gushed the rich juice in a stream red as blood. The party were often invited to taste the native products of the country, which were presented in almost embarrassing profusion; and the wine was always accompanied with assurances of its perfect harmlessness. It was "milder than milk," the peasants said; "and as to a headache, such a thing could never happen if one were to drink rivers of it."

Bordeaux is the great maritime city of this portion of France, and has large commercial importance. It is the great export city of red wine, to which it gives its name of Bordeaux. The situation of the city is on the bank of the Garonne river, and it is a very picturesque and busy place. Here our travelers spent several days, and had an opportunity of inspecting some of the enormous wine-cellars of Bordeaux, which are among the largest in the world. In one of these cellars ten thousand hogsheads of wine are stored.

There was much to interest General Grant at Bordeaux; but while there he received a message from the Spanish King, who was expecting him. Accordingly the party proceeded to Bairitz, where they rested for a night, and the next day crossed the frontier into Spain.

CHAPTER XVIII.

SPAIN AND PORTUGAL.

Along the Bayonne Route—Alfonso's Hospitality—Two Ex-Presidents Meet—Popular Demonstrations—The King to his American Guest—All, High and Low, vie in Honoring Him—Quiet at Madrid—The Attempt at Regicide—Refused to See a Bull Fight—Grant and Carnage—King Louis of Portugal—Knighthood Declined, the King's Hamlet Accepted—Grant and the Bulgarian Monarchy.

Entering Spain from France by the Bayonne route, the little town of Irun, just over the border, was the first to be reached by General Grant. Its neat railway station was draped with flags and bunting. A group of officers of the Royal Guard figured among the citizens. The village and country people flocked to town to see the distinguished visitor. Barriers kept them at a distance but they were eager for a glimpse. On alighting from the coach a General from the staff of Alfonso XII, saluted him and in the King's name welcomed him to the Iberian Peninsula. This officer stated that the King had directed him to place the royal car at the disposal of his guest. General Grant accepted the offer with thanks, and the train soon moved on.

The next point reached was San Sebastian, a city of very considerable military history and a stronghold of the Carlists. There he was met by the illustrious Emilio Castelar, orator, publisist statesman and patriot, ex-President of the Spanish Republic. To him the General said, truly, "Believe me, sir, the name of Castelar is especially honored in America." The popular demonstration in Grant's honor was enthusiastic and seemed to be participated in by the whole people. One would suppose the name of Grant familiar to and revered by the Spaniards of all classes.

Talosa and Vergara were soon reached. From the latter point the population was more dense and the stations more frequent. The party whirled along, everywhere met by demonstrations of respect, until Vittoria was reached where the General alighted, civil and military authorities greeted him and escorted him to his hotel. The King and his entire staff were at Vittoria at the time, in attendance upon the annual maneuvers of the Spanish army. In the evening the General took a stroll about town incognito.

The next morning the King received the General at the Aguntamiento, the residence of the Alcade. The King speaks English fluently, so they had no need of interpreters. He said he had long had a curiosity to see the General whose civil and military career were so familiar to him. "There is no man living," he said, "Whom Spain would more gladly honor." General Grant made fitting response, but indulged in no remarks of a general nature. At eleven o'clock both, with a retinue of nobles and high officials, started out to view the maneuvers of the troops. The display, a grand one, occured on the field made memorable in June 1813 by the surrender of Joseph Bonaparte and Jourdan by the allies under Wellington. The King and the General rode side by side, and the former pointed out the objects and places of interest to his companion. From time to time distinguished officers were introduced to the General by the King.

In the evening the General dined with the King. The next day was set for a grand review of the troops by the General. Had he been the hero of Spain he could not have been honored more highly. From the King and General Concha to the privates all seemed eager to pay him homage.

The next evening General Grant took the train for Madrid, where he spent some days in quietly visiting the places of interest "doing" Madrid in accordance with his personal taste. But there was soon a highly sensational incident—almost a tragic event. As the King was riding through a street known as Calle Major, a pistol was fired at him. Like the other would-be King-killers, of the period, the assassin missed his aim. The bullet cleft the air, and nothing more. The would-be assassin was a young cooper, Juan Moncasi by name, a member of the International society, or as Disraeli called it in "Lothaire," the "Mary Ann." At the time the shot was fired General Grant was standing at a window in the Hotel de Paris some distance off, but in full view of the royal cavalcade at the place of attack. He saw the flash of the pistol. He had already made his arrangements for starting for Lisbon at seven o'clock that evening, and could not stop to personally congratulate the King upon his escape. But to Senor Silvera, Minister of State, who called soon after and accompanied him to the railway station he expressed his sympathy, and regretted his inability to personally call upon his Majesty.

In bidding farewell to Spain it may be added that the General declined to witness a Bull fight. The grand review of an army was not much to his taste, but a brutal encounter between a man and a beast he declined to witness. In war he could go on his way undisturbed by carnage. He accepted it as a part of the inevitable. No General ever seemed more indifferent to suffering. A story is told illustrative of this characteristic which serves as the antipode of his refusal to attend a Bull fight. In the midst of a battle an Aide announced to him the death of General Ransom. His only remark was, "Who is in command?" General Sherman, when told the same news was loud and intense in his expressions of grief, although no warmer friend to the fallen chieftain than Grant. The latter had that imperturbility which passes for insensiblility often, but is really a totally different trait of character.

At Lisbon King Luis of Portugal paid our hero every mark of distinction. A grand dinner was given him. The palace was gaily trimmed with flags and the day was a festival throughout the city. His Majesty offered the General the highest decoration of Knight-hood known in the Kingdom. It was politely declined. The King was told by his honored guest that the laws of this country forbid officers to wear decorations, and although he was not now in office he preferred to respect the law. The King then offered him a copy of his translation of "Hamlet" into Portugese, which of course, the General accepted with many thanks.

AUSTRIA—MONTE PELINO.

THE MARMOLATA, FROM THE PASS OF ALLEGHE.

MONTE CIVITA.

Sketches in Austria.

The General paid a visit to Gibraltar while in its vicinity and about this time. He was received by the British military authorities there with befitting honors. In company with Lord Napier of Magdala he reviewed the whole of the troops in the British garrison, and, later in the day, witnessed a sham-fight. The display in both instances was magnificent. General Grant warmly praised the evolutions. He spoke in enthusiastic praise of the men and the officers.

On his return trip the General visited many points of interest in Spain, Cadiz, Grenada, Malaga, and the Alhambra hills, with their orange and cypress groves.

In this connection may be mentioned the linking by rumor of General Grant's name with the Bulgarian throne. It was late in November when the correspondent of the London *Standard* (a paper not given to sensational matter) at Philliopolis telegraphed that he had the highest authority for saying that General Grant had been proposed for the Bulgarian throne. That was probably true, but no formal steps were taken, so far as known, in that direction. In no public way, at least, did the General have occasion to notice the rumor. If he ever chatted on the subject, or referred to it in any way, the public is ignorant of the fact and doubtless always will be. The press of this country made it the occasion of

M

a good deal of pleasantry. It was never discussed seriously.

Under the provisions of the first and third articles of the treaty of Berlin, Bulgaria was constituted an autonomous principality, under the suzerainty of a Sultan with a Christian government and a national militia. The Prince was to be elected by the populace, the choice to be approved and confirmed by the Porte, and by England, France, Germany, Russia, Austria and Italy. No member of any reigning European dynasty was eligible to the position. The Bulgarian Nobles not unnaturally thought of General Grant as a suitable person for the office. It is safe to assume that he had no liking for the chief magistracy of that small, remote and uninteresting principality.

CHAPTER XIX.

GENERAL GRANT AND THE IRISH.

Arrival at Dublin—The General on the Irish—The Longest Speech of His Life—National Prosperity Discussed—The Council of Cork—Irish Cordiality Everywhere Else.

In the last chapters we have sketched the six months General Grant devoted to Northern and Southern Europe, among people unfamiliar with the English tongue, and where for the most part he enjoyed not only rest from public speaking, but public demonstrations such as his visit had occasioned in England and Scotland, and was destined to occasion in the far East. We are now to follow him to Ireland, the last European country visited by him, and where, with the one exception of Cork, he was received with honors worthy the man and the people.

Accompanied by General Noyes, as well as his usual party, the General arrived at Dublin, January 3, 1879. Again the "freedom of the city;" business was resumed. All Dublin was excited, and joined in showering honors upon the illustrious guest. The Lord Mayor, in presenting the freedom of the city, referred to the cordiality always existing between America and Ireland, and hoped that in America General Grant would do everything he could to help a people who sympathize with every American movement. The parchment, on which was engrossed the freedom of the city, was inclosed in an ancient, carved bog-oak casket.

General Grant appeared to be highly impressed by the generous language of the Lord Mayor. He replied: "I feel very proud of being made a citizen of the principal city of Ireland, and no honor that I have received has given me greater satisfaction. I am by birth the citizen of a country where there are more Irishmen, native born or by descent, than in all Ireland. When in office I had the honor—and it was a great one, indeed—of representing more Irishmen and descendants of Irishmen than does Her Majesty the Queen of England. I am not an eloquent speaker, and can simply thank you for the great courtesy you have shown me." Three cheers were given for General Grant at the close of his remarks, and then three more were added for the people of the United States.

Mr. Isaac Butt, the well known home-rule member of Parliament, now dead, speaking as the first honorary freeman of the city, congratulated General Grant on having consolidated into peace and harmony the turbulent political and sectional elements over which he triumphed as a soldier. His speech throughout was highly complimentary of the ex-President.

In the evening a grand banquet was given in honor of the ex-President, over two hundred guests being present. The Lord Mayor presided. General Noyes returned thanks for a toast to President Hayes' health. When General Grant's name was proposed, the company arose and gave the Irish welcome.

The ex-President made in response the longest speech of his life, speaking in a clear voice, and being listened to with rapt attention. He referred to himself and fellow citizens of Dublin, and intimated, amid much laughter and cheering, that he might return to Dublin one day and run against Barrington for Mayor, and Butt for Parliament. He warned those gentlemen that he was generally a troublesome candidate. Then passing to serious matters, the General said:

"We have heard some words spoken about our country —my country. before I was naturalized in another. We have a very great country, a prosperous country, with room for a great many people. We have been suffering for some years from very great oppression. The world has felt it. There is no question about the fact that, when you have forty-five millions of consumers such as we are, and when they are made to feel poverty, then the whole world must feel it.

"You have had here great prosperity because of our great extravagance and our great misfortunes. We had a war which drew into it almost every man who could bear arms, and my friend who spoke so eloquently to you a few moments ago lost a leg in it. You did not observe that, perhaps, as he has a wooden one in place of it.

"When that great conflict was going on, we were spending one thousand million dollars a year more than we were producing, and Europe got every dollar of it. It made for you a false prosperity. You were getting our bonds and our promises to pay. You were cashing them yourselves. That made great prosperity, and made producers beyond the real necessities of the world at peace. But we finally got through that great conflict, and with an inflated currency which was far below the specie you use here. It made our people still more extravagant. Our speculations were going on, and we still continued to spend three or four hundred millions of money per year more than we were producing.

"We paid it back to you for your labor and manufactures, and it made you apparently and really prosperous. We, on the other hand, were getting really poor, but being honest, however, we came to the day of solid, honest payment. We came down to the necessity of selling more than we bought. Now we have turned the corner. We have had our days of depression; yours is just coming on. I hope it is nearly over. Our prosperity is commencing, and as we become prosperous you will, too, because we become increased consumers of your products as well as our own. I think it safe to say that the United States, with a few years' more such prosperity, will consume as much more as they did. Two distinguished men have alluded to this subject—one was the President of the United States, and he said that the prosperity of the United States would be felt to the bounds of the civilized world. The other was Lord Beaconsfield, the most far-seeing man, the one who seems to me to see as far into the future as any man I know, and he says the same as President Hayes."

General Grant's speech created a profound sensation, and was loudly cheered during its delivery.

About this time the United States Consul at Cork addressed a letter to the Council, announcing that Grant would probably arrive in Cork within a few days. Mr. Tracy, a nationalist, proposed at the Council meeting that the letter should simply be marked "read," and that no action should be taken. Mr. Harris, a conservative, said: "It will be to the interest of our fellow-countrymen in the United States if a proper reception is accorded to General Grant, who represents the governing party in that country. There can be no personal antipathy to the gentleman himself; neither was there anything in the government of the ex-President objectionable to the Irish people nor unpleasant to the Irish in America. Probably General Grant would again be at the head of the United States, in which event it would be to the interest of our fellow-countrymen in America if proper recognition was given to General Grant on his arrival at Cork."

Mr. Barry, an extreme nationalist, said the ex-President had insulted the Irish people in America. He got up the "No Popery" cry there.

Mr. Tracy said it would be unbecoming for the Catholic constituency of Cork to welcome such a man. It would be ungenerous to refuse him hospitality if he deserved it, but he saw nothing in General Grant's career that called for sympathy from the Irish nation. He never thought of the Irish race as he thought of others, and he went out of his way to insult their religion.

Mr. Dwyer, an advanced nationalist, would not couple General Grant's name with America. The Irish who sought a refuge and a home in the United States had received kindness and attention from the American people. President Grant had never given them the same recognition as the other inhabitants. It would be an impropriety to pay any mark of respect personally to General Grant.

Messrs. McSweeny and Creedon, nationalists, spoke to the same effect, and with a great shout of "Aye," there being no dissenting voices, Cork refused to receive General Grant.

This action of the city of Cork produced a profound sensation throughout Ireland, the people looking at it as a violation of the rites of hospitality. General Grant smiled when told of the action of the Cork Councilmen, and said he was sorry the Cork people knew so little of American history.

The respectable liberals and conservatives of the city and county of Cork were indignant at the action of the clique in the Council who insulted ex-President Grant. An ex-Mayor of the city said: "The obstructionists who opposed a *cead mille failthe* to General Grant are not worth a decent man rubbing up against. It is a pity that the General has determined to return to Paris instead of visiting Cork (which determination was reached entirely independent of the Council indignity), where he would have received such an ovation from the self-respecting populace as would prove that the Irish heart beats in sympathy with America."

We return now to the actual movements of General Grant. After three days spent in seeing the interesting sights at Dublin, he pursued his journey, the popular enthusiasm everywhere intense. Reaching Ulster in due time, he was invested with citizenship once more, and made a speech, in which he said that no incident of his trip was more pleasant than accepting citizenship at the hands of the representatives of this ancient and honored city, with whose history the people of America were so familiar. He regretted that his stay in Ireland would be so brief. He had originally intended embarking from Queenstown direct for the United States, in which case he would have remained a much longer time on the snug little island; but, having resolved to visit India, he was compelled to make his stay short. He could not, however, he said in conclusion, return home without seeing Ireland and a people in whose welfare the people of the United States took so deep an interest. The actions of Cork seemed to stimulate the most cordial manifestations of honor in every other part of Ireland visited by General Grant. That discourtesy was due to a misapprehension of a speech made by General Grant during the last year of his Presidency at Des Moines, in which he made an earnest and forcible plea for the complete freedom of public schools from sectarian influences. It was one of the happiest efforts of his life in public speaking; but the Corkonian Alderman got the impression that he was a latter-day Oliver Cromwell. That episode served the good purpose of giving special emphasis to the sentiment of the Des Moines speech, also of stimulating Irish American patriots to a proper repudiation of Corkonian insolence and expression of genuine Irish enthusiasm for the hero of their admiration.

CHAPTER XX

IN INDIA.

THROUGH THE SUEZ CANAL—ENGLISH TREATMENT OF GRANT IN ASIA—ARCHITECTURE IN INDIA— THE CLIMATE—BOMBAY DURING THE REBELLION—THE MAHARAJAH OF JEYPORE—GENERAL GRANT, THE PRINCE OF WALES AND THE NAUCHT GIRLS—LORD LYTTON AND GENERAL GRANT— UNIVERSITY EXERCISES AT CALCUTTA—NATIVE PRINCES—OFF FOR SIAM.

Leaving Ireland the General made his way to Marseilles, *via* London and Paris, with very little and quite uneventful detention on the way. Leaving Paris January 21st he sailed for India from Marseilles two days later. He passed through the Suez Canal, and from the especial interest he had already taken in the project of connecting the two great oceans by canal at the Isthmus of Darien, it may well be supposed that the passage through the Suez possessed for him extraordinary importance. February 1st he left Suez for Bombay, reaching the latter city on the thirteenth day of that month, after an uneventful voyage, just as his voyages were all of them uneventful. From the day he left Philadelphia to the day he reached San Francisco his experiences at sea were all undiversified by any hairbreadth escapes, or the like. He was not even seasick.

The General spent six weeks "doing" India. To follow him day by day from the time he landed at Bombay to the time he left Singapore for Siam and beyond, would be tedious. It is proposed to go into details only so far as the same may serve to give a just and vivid idea of what our hero saw and experienced in that remarkable country, where British conquest and American Christianity have done so much in their different ways to revolutionize a nation by nature repellant of change.

Thus far it has been from the English that General Grant has received the most flattering attentions. Henceforth he is to breathe a somewhat different atmosphere, so far as concerns the British. In all Asia, with one German exception, to be noted and explained hereafter, the only approaches to disrespect were from Britons. In some cases the very fact that the natives about them were respectful almost to adoration, seemed to feed repugnance in the British residents, accustomed as they were to arrogant airs over the "heathen round about." But this surliness, for that was what it amounted to, did not manifest itself much in India. The different representatives-in-chief of the Home Government at the various cities visited vied in maintaining the policy pursued at all the points in England which the General had visited.

A vast multitude thronged the wharf at Bombay eager to catch a glimpse of the distinguished visitor. The leading British officers stationed there, civil and military, were on hand to welcome him, with an imposing escort of the Bombay volunteers, who presented arms, the band playing American airs.

To give an idea of architecture in India, and a glimpse of life there, where the problem is to guard against the excessive heat, we append a description of the Government House residence provided for the General at this city, and the surroundings, as described by one of the party in a letter to the New York *Herald:*

"The house is a group of houses. As you drive in the grounds through stone gates that remind you of the porter's lodge at some stately English mansions you pass through an avenue of mango trees, past beds of flowers throwing out their delicate fragrance on the warm morning air. You come to a one-storied house surrounded with spacious verandas. There is a wide state entrance covered with red cloth. A guard is at the foot, a native guard wearing the English scarlet, on his shoulders the number indicating the regiment. You pass up the stairs, a line of servants on either side. The servants are all Mohammedans; they wear long scarlet gowns, with white turbans; on the breast is a belt with an imperial crown for an escutcheon. They salute you with the grave, submissive grace of the East, touching the forehead and bending low the head, in token of welcome and duty. You enter a hall and pass between two rooms—large, high, decorated in blue and white—and look out upon the gardens below, the sea beyond, and the towers of Bombay. One of these rooms is the State dining-room, large enough to dine fifty people. The other is the State drawing-room. This house is only used for ceremonies, for meals, and receptions. You pass for one hundred paces under a covered way over a path made of cement and stone, through flower-beds and palm-trees, and come to another house. Here are the principal bedrooms and private chambers. This also is one story high, and runs down to the sea, so that you can stand on a balcony and throw a biscuit into the white surf as it combs the shore. These are the apartments assigned to General Grant and his wife. There are drawing-rooms, ante-rooms, chambers, the walls high, the floors covered with rugs and cool matting. As you pass in, servants, who are sitting crouched around on the floors, rise up and bend the head. You note a little group of shoes at the door and learn that in the East custom requires those in service to unslipper themselves before entering the house of a master. Another hundred paces and you come to another house, with wide verandas, somewhat larger than the General's. These are the guest-chambers and here a part of our party reside."

It was winter, yet judged by our standard of temperature, summer. It was not prudent to be out of doors during mid-day with uncovered head or any time while the sun was shining.

Bombay might well take an especial interest in the foremost General of our war, for during those four years that city enjoyed an unwonted prosperity. The arrest in the shipment of cotton from the South to England stimulated the Indian cotton trade wonderfully (and Bombay as the New Orleans of Hindoostan.) In 1860 its cotton export was only about $26,000,000, while during the four years of our great conflict it was four times that amount. The peace of Appomattox was followed by a financial panic in that far away commercial metropolis. The Parsee merchants were the especial losers by our peace. But they none the less cordially honored the hero of that peace when he came among them half a generation later. Numerous invitations were received from native rulers to visit their provinces. Most of these were declined, of course. The General, however, took in Jeypore, and was the guest of the Maharajah who is thus described:

"The Maharajah sent word that he would receive General Grant at 5. The Maharajah is a pious Prince, a devotee, and almost an ascetic. He gives seven hours a day to devotions. He partakes only of one meal. When he is through he plays billiards. He is the husband of ten wives. His tenth wife was married to him a few weeks ago. The court gossip is that he did not want another wife—that nine were enough—but in polygamous countries marriages are made to please families, to consolidate alliances, to win friendships, very often to give a home to the widows or sisters of friends. The Maharajah was under some duress of this kind, and his bride was brought home and is now with her sister brides behind the stone walls, killing time as she best can, while her lord prays and plays billiards. I asked one who knows something of Oriental ways what these poor women do whom destiny elevates to the couch of a King. They live in more than cloistered seclusion. They are guarded by eunuchs, and, even when ailing, cannot look in the face of the physician, but put their hands through a screen. I heard it said in Jeypore that no face of a Rajput Princess was ever seen by a European. These prejudices are respected and protected by the Imperial Government, which respects and protects every custom in India so long as the States behave themselves and pay tribute. In their seclusion the Princesses adorn themselves, see the Nautch girls dance, and read romances."

Reference is made to the Naucht girls above. It was there that this Oriental dance was performed for the pleasure of the General, but in a very different way from its performance for the delectation of the Prince of Wales. Writing on this subject, after news of the entertainment had reached London, and been the subject of gossip, M. D. Conway observes in a letter to the Baltimore *Gazette:*

"There is a quiet smile going around anent General Grant in India. The smile began in Calcutta, came to London via Paris, and it is only fair it should be passed on to America. Speaking of the Nautch dance at Jeypore, attended by General Grant, the *Herald* reporter says:

"The girls wore heavy garments embroidered," and adds: "The Nautch dance is meaningless. It is not even improper." The fact is the dance was made dull and respectable for the sake of the Grant party. When the Prince of Wales was out here and went to see the dance it was not considered necessary to be so careful, and the Nautch girls entered on their ballet in their usual costume, which above the waist consists only of jewels. They danced, too, for the Prince like mad! The Prince of Wales was "highly delighted" by the Nautch girls, and did not, like our ex-President, wear an expression of "resignation tinted with despair." The feeling which the Hindoos thus exhibited of the differences to be recognized between what is proper for a Prince and what for an American President may, after the smile has passed, suggest a thought to the political philosopher. Nobody here, not even the pious papers, called the Prince to account for countenancing the Nautch dance and its nudities; but, had General Grant been equally free and easy, the incident might have become a factor in the third terminology.

After the dancing the Prince and the General played a game of billiards, the latter being beaten. The party ceremony is worth recording. After a few memento presents, a servant bore in a small cup of gold and gems containing ottar of roses. The Maharajah, getting some of the perfume on his fingers, transferred it to Mrs. Grant's handkerchief. With another portion he passed his hands along the President's breast and shoulders. This was done to each of the party. The General then taking the perfume passed his hands over the Maharajah's shoulders. That ceremony betokens lasting friendship."

A tiger hunt was gotten up and participated in by some of the party, but the General has no taste for any sports of cruelty and did not join in chase, so it may be given the go-by here. He visited several schools and temples. He was interested in visiting the accessible places of historical interest, especially those connected with the ever memorable Sepoy mutiny. But nothing particularly remarkable is reported until Calcutta was reached. It is there that the Viceroy of India resides. That high and lucrative office is filled by Lord Lytton, so favorably known in poetical literature as "Owen Meredith." This son of the great novelist, Bulwer, is a gentleman of the finest culture and an enviable diplomatic reputation. The author of "Lucile" sent an urgent invitation to General Grant then at Bombay, to be his guest, delaying a trip of his own for that purpose. March 10th found the General there. A guard of honor met him. The streets were lined with policemen. He was taken to the Government house. That evening a state dinner was given by Lord Lytton in his honor. In his toast to the ex-President, the host referred to America as "the most 'go-ahead' representative of that good old sturdy stock in the little island in the Northern Seas, whose ideas are spreading in every part of the world." He referred to the office of President as the highest a citizen of a free country could hold. General Grant had now victories in peace and war. Like his classic namesake, he had seen men and cities in all parts of the world, enlarging the genius of a statesman by the experience of a traveler. The Viceroy hoped, when General Grant returned to 'the great empire' which he had once rescued and twice ruled, he would carry with him many kind recollections of India.

In a subsequent post-prandial speech, Lytton referred to his former residence in America as an attachee of the British Embassay under his uncle, Sir Henry Bulwer, and expressed the hope of revisiting this country. He would certainly find a warm welcome, for his genius as a poet is held in high esteem on this side of the Atlantic.

The annual convocation for conferring degrees of the University took place while General Grant was in Calcutta. The General, accompanied by Sir Ashley Eden, Lieutenant-Governor of Bengal, and Sir Alexander Arbuthnot, the Vice Chancellor, attended the convocation. The General and the Bishop of Calcutta sat on the Vice-Chancellor's right, and Sir Ashley Eden on the left. Degrees were conferred upon students from the various colleges throughout India, and the Vice-Chancellor made a speech, which contained some interesting references to education in India. "The present scheme of Indian education," said Sir Alexander, "came into operation the year of the mutiny, and the two and twenty years it had been in existence showed gratifying results." The speaker found reason for congratulation in the fact that the Senate had passed rules for the examination of female candidates, and that under these rules a Hindoo young lady had passed with high credit. There was an increasing desire among the young men of Bengal that their wives and daughters should be educated. In conclusion, Sir Alexander made the following allusion to the presence of General Grant:

"GENTLEMEN: Before I sit down I must ask permission to offer the respectful but cordial thanks of the University to the distinguished American soldier and statesman, who is seated on my right, for having honored this convocation by his presence. (Cheers.) In General Grant we see a conspicuous instance of that devotion to duty, that tenacity of purpose, that quiet but indomitable energy which characterizes the best men, not only of the Anglo Saxon, but of every race. (Loud cheers.) Alike to us who have long been engaged in the business of life, and to you who are now about to enter upon it, the career of General Grant furnishes a remarkable example of duties faithfully and efficiently discharged and of difficulties successfully overcome; and here let me remind you that there is no sphere of duty, however limited, no position in life, however humble, in which the contemplation of such an example is without its value. In the words of an eminent countryman of our illustrious visitor, in the words of an American poet who still lives to adorn the literature of his country, and who is held in honor wherever the English language is read:

We have not wings, we cannot soar,
But we have feet to scale and climb,

> By slow degrees, by more and more,
>   The cloudy summits of our time.
>
> The hights by great men reached and kept
>   Were not attained by sudden flight;
> But they, while their companions slept,
>   Were toiling upward in the night.
>
> Standing on what too long we bore,
>   With shoulders bent and downcast eyes,
> Let us discern, unseen before,
>   A path to higher destinies.
>
> Nor deem the irrevocable past
>   As wholly wasted, wholly vain,
> If, rising on its wrecks, at last
>   To something nobler we attain.

The only remaining feature of the sojourn in Calcutta worthy of mention, is the presentation to the General by the Viceroy of a class of native princes, who are now pensioners of the British government, their authority all gone. The decapitation of one who was not presented, and of his son who was, must suffice.

The son of the King of Oude wore a headdress shaped like a crown and covered with gold-foil and lace. The King lives in Calcutta, on an allowance of $600,000 a year. He does not come near the Government house himself. He is so fat that he cannot move about, except in a chair, besides, he is a kind of State prisoner on account of the supposed sympathies with the mutiny. The old King spends a good share of his income in buying animals. He has a collection of snakes, and is fond of a peculiar kind of pigeon. A pigeon with a blue eye will bring him a good fortune; and if one of his Brahmin priests tells him that the possession of such a bird is necessary to his happiness, he buys it. Recently he paid £1,000 for a pigeon on the advice of a holy Brahmin, who it was rumored, had an interest in the sale. Not long since the King made a purchase of tigers, and was about to buy a new and choice lot, when the Lieutenant Governor interfered and said his Majesty had tigers enough. My admiration for the Kingly office is so profound that I like it best in its eccentric aspects, and would have rejoiced to have seen so original a Majesty. But his Majesty is in seclusion with his snakes, his tigers, his pigeons, his priests and his women, and sees no one, and we had to be content with seeing his son. The Prince seemed forlorn with his bauble crown, his robes and his gems, and hid behind the pillars and in corners of the room, and avoided general conversation.

Not by any means the least interesting part of the visit at Calcutta, was the final interview between Lord Lytton and General Grant. They naturally chatted of our national capital where the Viceroy lived three years, and of changes wrought since then. That was in the last days of the great triumvirate, Webster, Clay and Calhoun. They talked of persons and things, treating also upon party politics in this country, the Viceroy remarking that he could not comprehend how an American who believes in his country, could sustain any policy that did not confirm and consolidate the results of the war. Whatever the merits of the war in the beginning, the end was to make America an Empire, to put our country among great nations of the earth, and such a position was now every American's heritage, and the defense of which should be his first thought.

The General had not intended to sail directly from India to Siam; but owing to the movements of the "Richmond," he visited Rangoon, British Burmah. It is a city, partly Indian and partly Chinese in its characteristics, with hardly enough individuality to justify us in lingering, and we hasten on to Siam.

CHAPTER XXI.

IN SIAM.

OUT OF THE BRITISH EMPIRE—SIAM, ITS CLIMATE, SOIL, RELIGION AND POPULATION — GRAND PREPARATIONS FOR GRANT—THE EX-REGENT A SCIENTIFIC GENTLEMAN—THE KING AND THE GENERAL MEET INFORMALLY—THE ROYAL TEMPLES — THE VICE-KING, ALSO A SCIENTIST — THE ROYAL ELEPHANT STABLE—AN ENTOMOLOGICAL DINNER— MORE NAUTCHING—FAREWELL INTERVIEW—A LONG CONVERSATION ON MANY SUBJECTS—GOOD-BYE LETTERS.

Hitherto, in all his journeyings our modern Ulysses has kept within the circle of European influence. He was no more on British soil in London than at Bombay. But now at length he is about to make the acquaintance of the independent Orient. His course lies towards Siam, called by the people themselves, *Muang Thai,* "kingdom of the free." Quite out of the ways of our latter-day civilization, he was by no means going among a barbarous people. The late king, Maha Mongkut, who died within a few weeks of General Grant's first election to the presidency, was no doubt the most learned sovereign of his day. Before pursuing our travels farther it may be of interest to glance at the country itself.

Siam proper, with all the country surrounding the Gulf of the same name, extends between the latitudes 6 deg. and 20 deg. north, and longitudes 98 deg. and 106 deg. east, measuring north and south nine hundred miles, and east and west, four hundred and twenty miles. It has a widely diversified climate and a remarkably rich soil, yielding a great variety of products. The people are Buddhists. Their sacred era is reckoned from his birth, nearly six hundred years before Christ, and their civil era from the establishment of the nation, something over a thousand years before this nation had an existence. The last census, taken twelve years ago, gave the population, or rather the adult males, who alone are registered, as eight millions. It is said that there is hardly a man or woman in the kingdom who can not read and write. The literature is voluminous, abounding especially in theological and poetical works. Instead of ten commandments, the Buddhists have five, namely, thou shalt not kill, steal, commit adultery, lie or get drunk, with love as the source and perfection of all virtues. In the arts, applied and decorative, they deserve no mean rank. In theory the government is a duarchy, in practice a monarchy. On the night the late king died, October 1st, 1868, the royal council, (*Senabawdee,*) elected his eldest son, Samdeteh Chowfa Chullalonkorn, to succeed him and another son, Prince George Washington, as second king. There was no disorder, nor any dissent.

The capital, Bangkok, has been called the Venice of the East. Perfect religious freedom is enjoyed. A species of slavery existed until January 1, 1872, when a system of gradual abolition was adopted, such as obliterated slavery from such of the Northern States as were once disgraced by that institution. The slaveholders were remunerated for their loss by a fund raised by general taxation. Such, in brief is the land which General Grant is now to visit.

The king laid down a programme in advance for the reception of his distinguished guest. It covered a period of seven days. It was not like the laws of the Medes and Persians, unalterable, but it was carried out, in the main. On the arrival of the party at Paknam a deputation of high dignitaries was to meet him, and in the name of his Majesty welcome him and convey him in the royal yacht to Bangkok. Officers of the foreign Department were to meet him off shore, and a military escort be in waiting at the wharf. The subsequent details were elaborately and gorgeously arranged. As the royal and princely barges moved from the landing the band (and the Siamese are very good musicians) struck up "Hail Columbia." The line of carriages was long. Without any tedious delay the General was conveyed to the palace of Hevang Saranrom, belonging to the second brother of the King and situated very near the palace of his Majesty. The young prince speaks English fluently, and escorted Mrs. Grant upon his arm in good Occidental rather than Oriental style. Until the next morning the guests were undisturbed by any calls or demands upon their time.

Before the audience with the King, which was set down for four o'clock, the General made several calls, the most interesting of which was upon the ex-Regent, a man who has passed the great land mark, three score years and ten, and who ruled the country during the minority of the present King. In the course of his conversation with General Grant he spoke of General Grant's policy having always been a pacific one, a friend to the nation. He observed that prosperity in a country like Siam, with many natural resources, depends upon the good faith of her neighbors, and of all the countries of the world. During his administration many of our inventions had been introduced into Siam; and he spoke of the gratitude which he always felt toward the United States for much of the present advancement of his country.

The royal reception was entirely informal. The King met the General much as one gentleman would another in this country, the conversation being on topics of mutual interest, every thing devoid of special ceremony. This brief interview over the General dined with the Foreign Minister. As the cooks are French importations there was nothing very peculiar about this or any other dinner. The Siamese agree with other civilized nations in giving the preference in culinary matters to Frenchmen.

In good season the second morning General Grant visited the royal temples which are discribed by one of the party as follows:

"The doors are of exquisite work of mother-of-pearl inlaid in ebony, window shutters of the same material, gold, silver, jewels of untold worth and of enormous size, in the Emerald Temple, called so from the image of Buddha on the top of the pyramidal gold throne in the centre under a canopy of gold reaching to the ceiling, and surrounded by figures, gilt, of Buddha, the fingers of which hold rings of precious stones, diamonds, emeralds, and rubies. The floor of this temple is made of blocks of brass, laid like bricks. One of the most extraordinary things in these temples is to see the offerings made—from ostrich eggs, elaborately carved, to clocks of old English make. Everything conceivable surrounds the golden pyramid. The walls are decorated with elaborate frescoes, representing scenes in the life of Guadama, and the rafters, painted red with black edges and gilt, give a rich appearance. We visited the various chapels, each under the guardianship of old women, who, with hair closely cut, and dressing in a costume much the same as men, with the addition of a yellow sash to make the distinction of sex."

It may be added that Gaudama sustains much the same relation to the Buddhist theology that Christ does to the Christian religion.

On this same day a visit was paid to the second King already referred to, who is merely a contingency, and an ornamental appendage; not so much like a Vice-President, who is a provision against death, as a Lieutenant-Governor, who has authority in the absence of the Governor. The salary of the Second King is $300,000. The General found him a scientific gentleman, more proud of his labratory than of anything else. In the palace he found an excellent bronze statue of himself, and other eminent rulers of the period, but in the secondary palace he found all the appliances of scientific research.

The next place of interest visited was the Royal Elephant Stable, kept by the King's uncle, a post of high honor it is, too. There they found the War Elephants, the sacred White

Elephant, which is of a *mouse* color, with white eyes. The latter is kept by a woman, and as he is rather vicious, and gets beyond control, no one attends upon him but this woman, of whom he is very fond. The King's servant ordered all the war trappings to be placed upon the Elephants that they might parade before the General for inspection.

A member of the party writing to a Philadelphia journal gives an account of a dinner given to the General by the Ex-Regent, April 15. He calls it an entomological dinner, partly on account of the scientific tastes and attainments of the host, but more because the heavy rains, unusual so early in the season, had driven the insects indoors. The country is noted for that kind of pest, its most serious annoyance. "They absolutely thronged the dinner table," he writes, adding, "were it not for the band that played during the dinner, I am sure the conversation would not have been found to be the most pious. Into your soup-plate a dozen mosquitoes would alight and die a rapid death, the champagne glass would be of value to any museum; but when they would crawl gently down the back of your neck, then all interest in the study of entomology would cease, and existence would be made exasperating. Most of the highest Siamese nobility were present, many speaking English fluently, and the great interest they all took in matters with us made the dinner pass, other circumstances excepted, most pleasantly. Siamese ladies, though they are not hidden like those of other Oriental races, do not appear in public on such occasions."

The same evening a reception on a large scale was given in the Saronrom Palace, the feature of its being a dance or Nautch. About twenty-two girls, with whitened faces, dressed in gilded, glittering dress, with golden head-pieces, helmet-shaped, looking like a pyramidal pagoda, danced rather gracefully and slowly in time with the music of a stringed violin band, twisted themselves into all contortions, until one would have thought that they must have been previously *boned*. This dance was kept up for at least two hours, and ended by a tragical performance of the dancers representing a scene in their mythology where one of them, with face covered with a blue mask, represented a giant and had a fight with a rival, ending in the latter's death. Generally entertainments of this kind continue all night, but it was brought within reasonable limits on this occcasion.

General Grant's farewell interview with the King occurred the next day. Her Royal Highness the Queen was present. She is, according to custom, the King's half sister. Her appearance is described as girlish. She talked a long time with Mrs. Grant. If some "Jenkins" had been present with the audacity to report their chat it would be a curious bit of literature, no doubt, but no such report was made. We can present, however, the report of the conservation between the General and the King, sent to the New York *Herald*, omitting only the surplusage:

The King said he hoped that the General had found everything comfortable for himself and party in the Saronrom Palace. The General said that nothing could be more agreeable than the hospitality of the Prince. The King said that he hoped that the General if he wanted anything, to see any part of Siam, go anywhere, or do anything, would express the wish, as he would feel it a great privilege to give him anything in his kingdom. General Grant said he appreciated the King's kindness and thanked him.

The King, after a pause, said that General Grant's visit was especially agreeable to him, because, not only in his own reign, but before, Siam had been under obligations to the United States. Siam saw in the United States not only a great but a friendly Power, which did not look upon the East with any idea of aggrandizement, and to whom it was always pleasant to turn for counsel and advice. More than that, the influence of most of the Americans who had come to Siam had been good, and those who had been in the Government's service had been of value to the State. The efforts of the missionaries to spread a knowledge of the arts and sciences, of machinery and of medicine, among the Siamese had been commendable. The King was glad to have the opportunity of saying this to one who had been the Chief Magistrate of the American people.

General Grant responded that the policy of the United States was a policy of non-intervention in everything that concerned the internal affairs of other nations. It had become almost a traditional policy, and experience confirmed its wisdom. The country needed all the energies of its own people for its development, and its only interest in the East was to do what it could to benefit the people, especially in opening markets for American manufactures. The General in his travels through India and Burmah, had been much gratified with the commendations bestowed upon American products; and, although the market was as yet a small one, he felt certain that the trade with the East would become a great one. There was the field at least, and our people had the opportunity. Nothing would please him more than to see Siam sharing in this trade. Beyond this there was no desire on the part of the American Government to seek an influence in the East.

The King said that nothing would please him more than the widest possible development of the commerce between Siam and America. The resources of Siam were great, but their development limited. Siam was like the United States in one respect, that it had a large territory and a small population, and the development of many sources of wealth that were known to exist had been retarded from this cause.

General Grant thought this difficulty might be met by the introduction of skilled labor, such, for instance, as mining experts from Nevada and California, who could prospect and locate mines, and labor-saving machinery, in which the Americans especially excelled.

The King assented to this, with the remark that the Siamese were a conservative people, and studied anything new very carefully before adopting it. Their policy in foreign relations had been a simple one,—peace with foreign Powers and steady development of the country. Siam was a small country, with limited resources, and she knew that she could not contend with the great foreign Powers. Consequently she always depended upon the justice and good will of foreign Powers. This sometimes led to their appearing to consent or to submit to some things which, under other circumstances and by other and greater nations, would not be endured. In the end, however, it worked right, and Siam, looking back over her relations with the Great Powers, found, on the whole, no reason for regret. In the main these relations had been for the good of the Siamese people. From the foreign Powers Siam had always received encouragement.

An allusion was made to the large Chinese population in Siam, and the King asked General Grant about the Chinese in America. The General said that there had been a large emigration of Chinese to the United States; that they brought with them many of the best qualities of laborers, but there was an objection in the minds of many good people at home to their arriving, as they did, in a condition of practical slavery.

The King asked whether the Chinese brought their wives and children to America and established any domestic ties with the country.

The General said that this was one of the difficulties,—one that most offended the moral sense of the people at home, the absence of domestic ties. This, and the condition of servitude in which they came, were the only objections that had any standing against the Chinese. As laborers they were good, and there were many fine points in their favor, many reasons why their labor was a benefit to the country with so much to develop as the United States.

The King said the same was practically true of the Chinese in Siam. They did not bring their wives and children, which was an objection. But they had many admirable qualities. He then asked whether the Chinese paid any taxes to the support of the Government.

General Grant answered that in America there could be no tax upon labor, and that there could be no distinction between the labor of the Chinaman and the labor of another race. What the State laws in States like California provided he was not aware, but his impression, as far even as California is concerned, was that the Chinaman paid nothing to the Government in the way of taxation. A few large merchants in San Francisco paid taxes on their property. This, however, would not be regarded as a special hardship, if there were no slavery and the laborers came with their families.

The conversation then passed to the industrial resources of Siam, and how they would be affected by closer relations with other Powers. The General said that it would be well for Siam to have Embassies or diplomatic relations with other nations, and he asked why it would not be a good thing for Siam to send an Embassy to the United States.

The King said he was anxious to carry out this idea, but there was a question of money concerned. Siam could not afford to keep Embassies on the same scale as the greater and richer nations. He had written to the United States Government offering to send an Embassy, and his action would depend upon the answer of the American authorities.

The General said he was not in office, was a simple private citizen, without authority, but he felt sure that the Government would receive any Embassy his Majesty chose to send with the utmost cordiality.

The King was pleased with this assurance, and said he had no doubt of the friendliest feeling toward Siam on the part of the American people.

The General asked whether it was not possible for the King to visit the United States and see the country. Such a visit would have a good effect, and he himself would be delighted to have the opportunity of entertaining his Majesty in the United States and returning some of the hospitalities he was now enjoying.

The King thanked the General for the invitation, but said a King of Siam was King for life. He did not have the felicity which had fallen upon the General of being able after a term of years to lay down office. So long a journey was impossible, and he was so young when the crown devolved upon him that he did not have the opportunity of foreign travel which had been given to Princes of other countries. He was sorry this had not been possible, as he desired nothing so much as to see other nations, and more especially the United States. He had made a visit to India, and was much interested in that country.

The General referred to India as a most interesting country. The talk then ran as to travel in India, the King asking the General as to his route and the cities he had seen. "In India," said the General, "you see one nation governing another. In Siam you see an Oriental nation governing itself. That was what especially interested him in Siam, and the success of the Government here, its enlightenment and progress, were most gratifying. He had seen nothing in the East more so."

General Grant then referred to education in the United States and to the fact that the Siamese Government had sent some of its young men to Germany and England for education. He suggested to his Majesty that it would be well to send some of these young men to American colleges. Other nations had done so, ruling families in Europe as well, notably the Chinese and Japanese. We had splendid schools in the United States, and the young men would return home with a better idea of the American people and the country. The King might depend upon these young men having the best reception; not merely a good education and careful training, but every personal courtesy.

The King said that he had sent several young men to England and Germany. He had intended sending several to the United States. Circumstances prevented his doing so. The Government had done as much in this way as it could afford at present. When the question arose again he would remember what the General had said on the subject.

It must be conceded that both the King and the General talked like thoroughly sensible men.

This chapter cannot be better closed than by giving the following correspondence, which explains itself:

GRAND PALACE, BANGKOK, April 20, 1879.

MY DEAR GENERAL GRANT: I have received your kind telegram on leaving Siam, and was very much pleased to hear that you were satisfied with your reception.

Your reception was not all I could have wished, for I had not sufficient notice to enable me to prepare much that I desired to prepare, but the good nature of your Excellency and Mrs. Grant has made you excuse the dificiencies.

You will now pass on to wealthier cities and more powerful nations, but I depend on your not forgetting Siam, and from time to time I shall write to you, and hope to receive a few words in return.

I shall certainly never forget the pleasure your visit has given me, and shall highly prize the friendship thus inaugurated with your Excellency and Mrs. Grant.

I send my kind regards to Mr. Borie, wishing him long life, health and happiness, and with the same wish to yourself and Mrs. Grant and your family, I am your faithful friend, CHULALONKORN, King of Siam.

To GENERAL GRANT.

UNITED STATES STEAMER ASHUELOT,
NEAR SHANGHAI, May 16, 1879.

To His Majesty, The King of Siam—Dear Sir: Just before leaving Hong Kong for Shanghai I received your very welcome letter of the 20th of April, and avail myself of the first opportunity of replying. I can assure you that nothing more could have been done by your Majesty and all those about you to make the visit of myself and party pleasant and agreeable. Every one of us will retain the most pleasant recollections of our visit to Siam, and of the cordial reception we received from yourself and all with whom we were thrown in contact.

I shall always be glad to hear from you and to hear of the prosperity and progress of the beautiful country over which you rule with so much justice and thought for the ruled.

My party are all well and join me in expression of great regards for yourself and Cabinet, and wishes for long life, health, and happiness to all of you, and peace and prosperity to Siam. Your friend, U. S. GRANT.

CHAPTER XXII.

CHINA AND THE CELESTIALS.

CHINESE ADDRESS OF WELCOME—ARRIVED AT CANTON—FIREWORKS, MILITARY PARADE AND POPULAR ENTHUSIASM—A CELESTIAL BULLETIN—DRINKING TEA WITH THE VICEROY OF CANTON—INTERESTING CORRESPONDENCE—RECEPTION AT TIENTSIN—AT PEKIN—THE PRINCE KUNG AND THE LOOCHOO ISLANDS—TWO IMPORTANT ADDRESSES, AND THE GENERAL'S RESPONSES—MORE HONORS AT TIENTSIN.

Leaving Siam General Grant steered his course for China, touching first at Saigon. His arrival was April 25th. The Governor of French Cochin China, Rear-Admiral LaFond, invited him to be his guest at the Government House. The next evening a public levee was given there in his honor, after which the voyage was resumed. Hong Kong was the next port of debarkation. There he found his old friend Mosby and others in waiting. A few days only could be given to Hong Kong, but the time was well improved. A deputation of Chinese presented him with the following address:

"*To General Ulysses S. Grant, late President of the United States of America, and Commander-in-Chief of the United States Army.*

"SIR: On the occasion of your honoring Hong Kong with your presence, we, the undersigned, on behalf of the Chinese community, approach you to give you a hearty welcome, and beg to present you an address expressive of our high esteem and respect for you. During your Presidency your great name and noble deeds were known far and wide, and by the carrying out of a just policy you commanded admiration and respect from all classes of people under your rule. We have been delighted to find that in international questions you have shown a spirit of impartiality and fairness, treating Americans and foreigners alike, and the Chinese who have been trading in the United States have sung, and continue to sing, praises of the many good actions done by you while in office.

"We had longed to see you, but, being far away, we were hitherto not permitted to realize our wish. Now that you have favored us with a visit we avail ourselves of the opportunity to present you with a scroll inscribed with these four words, "Benefit to Chinese People," which we hope may serve as a souvenir of your interview with the Chinese community of Hong Kong.

"Signed by Lee Ting, Ho Amei, Lee Tuck Cheong, and ninety others."

General Grant said:

"Gentlemen, I am very happy to meet so many representatives of the Chinese community in Hong Kong, and for the kind words of your address accept my thanks. I have looked forward for a long time to my visit to China, and am pleased to see, as I have seen in Hong Kong, that the Chinese are a thrifty, industrious and intelligent people. I have no other wish than that between the two peoples there shall be harmony and the best relations, and in this spirit I accept your address and the beautiful memento which accompanies it, and thank you for your good wishes."

The real tour of China began, however, at Canton, where he arrived May 6th. That great city is on Pearl river, thirty miles from the coast. At the seaboard a gun-boat met him, by order of the Viceroy, and escorted him to the city. All along the journey, on both banks of the noble stream, the people made great demonstrations of welcome. Guns were fired, the military paraded, and the scene was absolutely inspiring. It was evening when Canton was reached, and the display of fireworks was simply bewildering. The next day a grand parade of troops took place, business being suspended. Extra bulletins had duly prepared the public mind for this ovation. One of them reads, being translated:

"We have just heard that the King of America, being on friendly terms with China, will leave America early in the third month, bringing with him a suite of officers, etc., all complete on board the ship. It is said that he is bringing a large number of rare presents with him, and that he will be here in Canton about the 6th or 9th of May. He will land at the Tintsy ferry, and will proceed to the Viceroy's palace by way of the South gate, the Fantai's Ngamun and the Waning Street. Viceroy Lan has arranged that all the mandarins shall be there to meet him, and a full Court will be held. After a little friendly conversation he will leave the Viceroy's palace, and visit the various objects of interest within and without the walls. He will then proceed to the Roman Catholic Cathedral, to converse and pass the night. It is not stated what will then take place, but notice will be given."

This programme was carried out in spirit and letter. The reception at the Viceroy's palace was an interesting occasion. Conversation was of course awkward, brief, and formal, being entirely through interpreters. The drink served was tea, which was served in the peculiar manner of the country, namely, in two cups, one upon the other and forming, together, a globe, the upper hemisphere being useful in retaining the aroma of the tea, and in keeping the leaves back as you drink, for the brewing is done in the cups. The flavor is much better than it can be on our tea-pot plan of brewing. But the bill of fare, a curiosity in its way, contained many things besides the national beverage. Of this part of the entertainment and what followed a member of the party wrote:

"The food was all sweetmeats, candied fruits, walnuts, almonds, ginger, cocoanuts, with cups of tea and wine. The Viceroy with his chopsticks helped the General. This is true Chinese courtesy, for the host to make himself the servant of his guest. Then came a service of wine—sweet champagne and sauterne—in which the Viceroy pledged us all, bowing to each guest as he drank. Then, again, came tea, which in China is the signal for departure, an intimation that your visit is over. The Viceroy and party arose and led them to their chairs (the carriages of the occasion.) Each one was severally and especially saluted as they entered their chairs; and as they filed off under the trees, their coolies dangling them on their shoulders, they left the Viceroy and his whole court, with rows of mandarins and far-extending lines of soldiers in an attitude of devotion, hands held together toward the forehead and heads bent, the soldiers with arms presented. The music, real, banging, gong-thumping Chinese music, broke out, twenty-one guns were fired, so close that the smoke obscured the view, and they plunged into the sea of life through which they had floated, and back again, through one of the most wonderful sights ever seen, back to their shady home in the American Consulate."

Wonderful as had been previous receptions General Grant had never at that time been the recipient of such a stupendous ovation as that at Canton. No less than two hundred thousand people joined in the popular welcome, and the official honors were such as no foreigner had ever before enjoyed in China. This part of the narrative may best be closed by giving the correspondence which passed between the Viceroy of Canton and the General. It explains itself, and runs thus:

"To His Excellency, the Late President:

"It has been a high honor and a source of the deepest satisfaction to myself, the high provincial authorities and the gentry and people of Canton, that Your Excellency, whom we have so long desired to see, has been so good as to come among us.

"Upon learning from you of your early departure, while I dared not interfere to delay you, I had hoped, in company with my associates, to present my humble respects at the moment of your leaving. I refrained from doing so in obedience to your command.

"I have ventured to send a few trifles to your honored wife, which I hope she will be so kind as to accept.

"I trust that you both will have a prosperous journey throughout all your way, and that you both may be granted many years and abundant good. Should I ever be honored by my sovereign with a mission abroad, it will be my most devout prayer and earnest desire that I may meet you again.

"I respectfully wish you the fulness of peace.

Liu Kun."

To which General Grant replied:

United States Steamer Ashuelot,
Near Shanghai, China, May 16, 1879.

"His Excellency the Viceroy of Kwangtung and Kwangh..

"*Dear Sir:* Before leaving Hong Kong for more extended visits through the Celestial Empire, I was placed in possession of your very welcome letter giving expression to the best wishes of Your Excellency and of all the high officials in Canton for myself and mine. Since then it has been my good fortune to visit Swatow and Amoy, both, I understand, under Your Excellency's government, and have received at each the same distinguished reception accorded at Canton. Myself and party will carry with us from China the most pleasant recollections of our visit to the country over which you preside, and of the hospitatities received at your hands.

"Mrs. Grant desires to thank you especially for the beautiful specimens of Chinese work which you presented to her. With the best wishes of myself and party for your health, long life and prosperity, and in hopes that we may meet again, I am your friend. U. S. GRANT."

General Grant next visited Shanghai where he remained only two days. The time was occupied with festivals and pageantry, culminating in the celebration and reception by the Governor and Council. As the General and party came to the spot selected for landing, the banks of the river were thronged with Chinamen; at least one hundred thousand. Upon landing Mr. Little, Chairman of the Municipal Council presented the illustrious General to the Chinese Governor, who had come to do his part in the reception. The Governor was accompanied by a delegation of mandarins of high rank. The band played 'Hail Columbia,' and after the music and cheering ceased, Mr. Little advanced and read the following address:

SHANGHAI, May 17, 1870.

"To General U. S. GRANT.

"*Sir:* On behalf of this community I have the honor to welcoming you to Shanghai. In this, the easternmost commercial settlement of the continent the lines that unite the old and new worlds meet, and here we on the eastern edge of the oldest empire in the world appropriately greet an illustrious representative of the great Republic of the New World.

"Devoted as we are to trade, we have little to show that is of interest to the ordinary traveler. But as the head for two periods of a great cosmopolitan, commercial state, we trust that you will find something to interest you in this small commercial republic, itself as cosmopolitan as the great country from which you come.

"We thank you for coming to visit us. We trust that you will find that we have done all in our power to make your visit pleasant. We wish for you a future as happy and distinguished as your past, and that after you leave us you will remember with pleasure this little band of self-governed representatives of all States, united in peaceful pursuits, and furthering, we believe, not without success, the cause of progress in this country.

"I have the honor to be, sir, on behalf of the foreign community of Shanghai, your obendient servant,

R. W. LITTLE,
Chairman of the Committee."

After a moment's pause, General Grant said:

"LADIES AND GENTLEMEN:—I am very much obliged to you for the hearty welcome which you have paid me, and I must say that I have been a little surprised, and agreeably surprised. I have now been a short time in the country of which Shanghai forms so important a part in a commercial way, and I have seen much to interest me and much to instruct me. I wish I had known ten years ago what I have lately learned. I hope to carry back to my country a report of all I have seen in this part of the world, for it will be of interest and possibly of great use. I thank you again for the hearty welcome you have given me."

Fireworks, military parades and every kind of demonstration of honor followed each other in quick succession. Nothing was wanting to complete the tribute of admiration to the famous visitor and nothing occurred to mar the grandeur and pleasure of the occasion.

From here the General's course was toward Teintsin, where another gorgeous reception awaited him. It was at once official and popular. The Government and the governed seemed to vie in paying honor to him whom all delighted to honor. It was there the great Viceroy of China, Li Hung-Chaing met him. He sought many occasions to cultivate General Grant's acquaintance. Of the Viceroy, in this connection, Mr. J. Russell Young wrote:

"The great Viceroy, had taken the deepest interest in the coming of General Grant. He was of the same age as the General. They won their victories at the same time, the Southern rebellion ended in April, the Taeping rebellion in July, 1865. While General Grant was making his progress in India, the Viceroy followed his movements, and had all the particulars of the journey translated. As soon as the General reached Hong Kong, our Consul, Judge Denny, conveyed a welcome from the Viceroy. When questions were raised as to the reception of the General in Tientsin, the Viceroy ended the matter by declaring that no honor should be wanting to the General, and that he himself would be the first Chinaman to greet him in Tientsin and welcome him to the chief province of the empire. Between General Grant and the Viceroy friendly relations grew up, and while in Tientsin they saw a great deal of each other. The Viceroy had said that he did not care merely to look at, or even to make his acquaintance, but to know him well and talk with him. The Viceroy is known among the most advanced school of Chinese statesmen, anxious to introduce all the improvements of the Western world, to strengthen and develop China. This subject so dear to him was one that the General has, whenever he has met Chinese statesmen, tried to impress upon their minds—the necessity of developing their country, and of doing it themselves."

The General formed a high opinion of the Viceroy as a statesman of resolute and far-seeing character. A day or two after the General's arrival a ceremonial dinner was given in the temple. The hour was noon, and the Viceroy invited several guests to meet the General. The dinner was a princely affair. Before it ended, one of the party on behalf of the Viceroy, arose and read this speech:

"GENTLEMEN: It has given me great pleasure to welcome you as my guests to-day, more especially as you aid me in showing honor to the distinguished man who is now with us. General Grant's eminent talents as a soldier and a statesman, and his popularity while chief ruler of a great country, are known to us all. I think that it may be said of him now, as it was said of Washington a century ago, that he is "first in war, first in peace, and first in the hearts of his countrymen." His fame, and the admiration and respect it excites, are not confined to his own country, as the events of his present tour around the world will prove, and China should not be thought unwilling to welcome such a visitor. I thank the General for the honor he has conferred upon me. I thank you all, gentlemen, for the pleasure you have given me to-day, and I now ask you to join me in drinking the health of General Grant, and wishing him increasing fame and prosperity."

The Viceroy and all his guests arose and remained standing while Mr. Detring read this speech. At the close, the Viceroy lifted a glass of wine, and bowing to the General, drank the toast. General Grant then arose and said:

"YOUR EXCELLENCY AND GENTLEMEN OF THE CONSULAR CORPS: I am very much obliged to you for the welcome I have received in Tientsin, which is only a repetition of the kindness shown to me by the representatives of all nations since I came within the coasts of China. I am grateful to the Viceroy for the especial consideration which I have received at his hands. His history as a soldier and statesman of the Chinese Empire has been known to me, as it has been known to all at home who have followed Chinese affairs, for a quarter of a century. I am glad to meet one who has done such great service to his country. My visit to China has been full of interest. I have learned a great deal of the civilization, the manners, the achievements, and the industry of the Chinese people, and I shall leave the country with feelings of friendship towards them, and a desire that they may be brought into relations of the closest commercial alliance and intercourse with the other nations. I trust that the Viceroy will some time find it in his power to visit my country, when I shall be proud to return, as far as I can, the hospitality I have received from him. Again thanking your Excellency for your reception, and you, gentlemen of the Consular corps, for your kindness, I ask you to join with me in a toast to the prosperity of China and the health of the Viceroy."

Enough has been presented to give an idea of the reception at Tientsin. From there the party departed by "Mandarin boat," for Pekin, which was reached after a tedious journey of about one hundred and twenty miles. This city also

P

seemed to be wholly given to joy over the great occasion. Foreigners and natives, high and low, joined in the tribute of admiration. The Emperor himself is only a boy in his digits, and took no part in anything; but the Prince Regent, Prince Kung, was unwearied in his attentions. As soon as he knew that General Grant was to visit China, which was while he was in Paris, he took measures to secure for him every honorable attention. The motive actuating him was not entirely disinterested. The Prince wanted to enlist General Grant's sympathy and assistance in the settlement of the difficulty between China and Japan, growing out of the seizure of the Loochoo Islands by the latter. The General could not refuse to listen, and would gladly have mediated between the two nations; but he could not enter formally upon the functions of an umpire. He tried to infuse into both governments the spirit of arbitration. He talked freely on the subject, and without becoming entangled in the meshes of the dispute, or accomplishing any decisive results he extended a wholesome influence and acquitted himself with very admirable credit. The subject was first brought up by the Viceroy at Tientsin, who introduced it again when the General returned from Pekin and proceeded to Japan. Several visits were exchanged between the Prince and the General. He visited many places of interest, in fact, all the places thereabouts, acquiring quite an accurate conception of Chinese civilization. Two addresses were presented to him which deserve preservation here, in connection with the General's replies. The first was from the American residents in Pekin, the other from the students of the college established to teach the English language and the Occidental civilization. The President of the College, Dr. Martin, is an American. The first of these addresses is as follows:

"SIR: Twenty years ago the American flag for the first time entered the gates of this ancient capital. For the greater part of that time your countrymen have been residing here under its protecting folds, and it is with feelings of no ordinary type that we gather ourselves beneath its shadow this day to welcome your arrival; because to you, sir, under God, it is due that its azure field had not been rent in fragments and its golden stars scattered to the winds of heaven. Having borne that banner through a career of victory which finds few parallels in the pages of history, it was your high privilege to gather around it in a new cemented Union the long discordant members of our national family. Occupying the most exalted position to which it was possible for you to be elevated by the voice of a grateful people, your strength was in the justice and moderation of your administration, a force more potent than that of armed cohorts. After conferring on our country these inestimable benefits, as its leader in war and its guide in the paths of peace, we reflect with pride that you have shown the world how a great man can descend from a lofty station and yet carry with him the homage of his people and the admiration of mankind. As you travel from land to land, everywhere welcomed as the citizen of a wider commouwealth than that of our native country, we cannot forget that your visits to their shores possess an international character of which it is impossible to divest them. You are honored as the highest representative of our country who has ever gone beyond her borders, and America is the more respected for having given birth to such a son. Your presence here to-day directs the attention of this venerable empire to the great republic from which you come. It will also have the effect of turning the eyes of our countrymen towards the teeming millions of Eastern Asia; and fervently do we trust that it will help to impress them with the obligations of justice and humanity in their dealings with the people of China. Your antecedents, sir, leave us in no doubt as to the policy that would meet your approval. Hoping that your influence may contribute to the adjustment of difficulties which threaten to react so disastrously on American interests in China, and that thereby you will add another to the many laurels that crown your brow, we hail your visit as both opportune and auspicious, and again with one heart we bid you welcome to the capital of China.

"W. A. P. Martin, H. Blodget, D. C. McCoy, H. B. Morse, C. C. Moreno, J. H. Pyke, W. F. Walker, H. H. Lowry, J. H. Roberts, W. C. Noble, Chester Holcombe.

"*Pekin, June* 3, 1879."

The General said he was always glad to meet his fellow countrymen, and the kind words in which he had been welcomed added to the pleasure which such a meeting afforded in Pekin. The Americans were a wonderful people, for you found them everywhere, even here in this distant and inaccessible capital. He was especially pleased with the allusion in the address to the fact that in America a career was possible to the humblest station in life. His own career was one of the best examples of the possibilities open to any man and every man at home. That feature in America he was proud to recognize, for it was one of the golden principles of our government. The General again thanked the delegation for their kindness, wished them all prosperity in their labors in China, and a happy return to their homes where he hoped some day to meet them.

The second address, especially worthy of preservation, referred to above, was as follows:

"*General U. S. Grant, Ex-President of the United States:*

Sir: We have long heard your name, but never dreamed that we would have an opportunity to look on your face. Formerly the people of your Southern States rebelled against your government and nearly obtained possession of the land, but, through your ability in leading the national forces, the rebel chief was captured and the country tranquilized. Having commanded a million of men and survived a hundred battles, your merit was recognized as the highest in your own land, and your name became known in every quarter of the globe. Raised to the Presidency by the voice of a grateful people, you laid aside the arts of war and sought to achieve the victories of peace. The people enjoyed tranquility, commerce flourished, manufactures revived, and the whole nation daily became more wealthy and powerful. Your achievements as a civil ruler are equally great with your military triumphs. Now that you have resigned the

Presidency, you employ your leisure in visiting different parts of the world, and the people of all nations and all ranks welcome your arrival. It requires a fame like yours to produce effects like these. We, the students of this college, are very limited in our attainments, but all men love the wise and respect the virtuous. We, therefore, feel honored by this opportunity of standing in your presence. It is our sincere hope that another term of the Presidency may come to you, not only that your own nation may be benefited, but that our countrymen resident in America may enjoy the blessings of your protection.

"WANG FENGTSAR, tutor in Mathematics.
"WEN HSII, tutor in English.
"NA SAN, tutor in English.
"On behalf of the students of Tunguon College.
"*Kwang Sii*, 5 *y*. 4 *m*. 16 *d*.—*June* 5, 1879."

The General in response, said:

"GENTLEMEN: I am much obliged to you for your welcome and for the compliments you pay me. I am glad to meet you and see in the capital of this vast and ancient empire an institution of learning based upon English principles, and in which you can learn the English language. I have been struck with nothing so much in my tour around the world as with the fact that the progress of civilization— of our modern civilization—is marked by the progress of the English tongue. I rejoice in this fact, and I rejoice in your efforts to attain a knowledge of English speech and all that such a knowledge must convey. You have my warmest wishes for your success in this and in all your undertakings, and my renewed thanks for the honor you have shown me."

Although the second visit to Tientsin was a matter of necessity and brief, it seemed that the disposition to honor the modern Ulysses had not expended itself by any means, and the time was fully occupied with fetes, receptions and honors of various kinds. The Viceroy took especial pains to show General and Mrs. Grant such attentions as the Oriental traditions did not call for. He showed an independence of precedents which was refreshing. "There was probably nothing," writes one of the party, "more notable than the entertainment given to Mrs. Grant by the wife of the Viceroy on the last night of the General's stay in Tientsin. The principal European ladies in the colony were invited. Some of these ladies had lived in Tientsin for years, and had never seen the wife of the Viceroy—had never seen him except through the blinds of the window of his chair. The announcement that the Viceroy had really invited Mrs. Grant to meet his wife, and European ladies to be in the company, was even a more transcendent event than the presence of General Grant. Society rang with a discussion of the question which, since Mother Eve introduced it to the attention of her husband, has been the absorbing theme of civilization—what shall we wear? The question was finally decided in favor of the resources of civilization. The ladies went in all the glory of French fashion and taste." They came back from the Viceregal dinner at about eleven at night, and General Grant and party went immediately on board the

"Ashuelot." Here the farewells to kind friends were spoken, and it was with sincere regret that they said farewell. And it was an adieu not only to pleasant chance acquaintances, but to China, for now the "Richmond" is to proceed northward to Japan, the last foreign land visited by General Grant in his tour around the world.

JAPAN—A JAPANESE BED.

JAPAN—DINNER GIVEN BY A JAPANESE MINISTER.

CHAPTER XXIII.

JAPAN.

SUMMER IN JAPAN—THE CHINESE WALL—CHRISTIAN MISSIONS—A DAIMIO FOR GUIDE—BRILLIANT RECEPTION—MORE ADDRESSES—AT YOKOHAMA —BY RAIL TO TOKIO—IMPERIAL AUDIENCE— THE FOURTH OF JULY AT TOKIO—IN THE COUNTRY—PRIVATE LETTER FROM THE GENERAL— JAPANESE ARCHITECTURE — THE CABINET— FAREWELL ADDRESSES—THE LEAVE-TAKING AT YOKOHAMA—OFF FOR AMERICA.

The Summer of 1879, from June 21, to September 3, was spent by General Grant in Japan, the most enterprising, progressive and prosperous portion of Asia. Being in refreshing proximity to the North Pole *via* Behrings Straits, it was an excellent summer resort.

The "Richmond" came to anchor only twice more in the China Sea, before reaching Nagasaki, the first and with the exception of Yokohama, the only Japanese port visited. The first stopping place was at the point where the great wall of China comes down to the sea. That marvelous public work, the boundary "fence" between China and the Mongolia of the Tartars, is 1,250 miles in length. Its average width at the surface is from twenty to twenty-five feet. At the base it varies from forty to a hundred. It is made of stone and brick, and, considering that twenty centuries have been testing its workmanship, the work was well done. The late Secretary Seward estimated that the labor expended on that attempt to keep off the Northern hordes, would have built the Pacific railroad. General Grant went farther. "I believe," he said, "that the labor expended on this wall could have built every railroad in the United States, every canal and highway and most if not all of our cities." The story is that millions of workmen were employed on the wall, and that the work lasted for ten years.

Having inspected the Eastern extremity of the Chinese wall the party proceeded to Chefoo, the summer resort of the foreigners on the Chinese Coast, who can afford a luxury of that kind. The "Ashuelot" had preceded the "Richmond," and announced the coming of General Grant. Every thing was in readiness for his reception on a grand scale. Salutes were fired, buildings decorated and fire works touched off. Midnight of the day on which the "Richmond" came to anchor it steamed out for Nigasaki, where, for the second time, the party trod in the foot prints of Francis Xavier, the bright and morning star of modern missions, whom Protestants no less than his fellow Catholics, unite in revering. In nearing the port, the "Richmond" passed the worse than Tarpean rock, from which no less than thirty-seven thousand converts to Christianity were hurled to instant death in the sea below. All that has gone by now, and Japan seems disposed to consider favorably the religion of Western civilization.

It was morning when the port was reached. The wharf was lined with an eager multitude of sight-seers, craning their neck sand straining their eyes to catch a glimpse of the illustrious visitor. The American Consul and representatives of the Japanese Government presently came on board. Prince Dati said that he had been commanded by the Emperor to meet General Grant on his landing, to welcome him in the name of His Majesty, and to attend upon him as the Emperor's personal representative so long as the General remained in Japan. The value of this compliment can be understood when you know that

Prince Dati is one of highest noblemen in Japan. He was one of the leading daimios, one of the old feudal barons who, before the revolution, ruled Japan and had powers of life and death in his own dominions.

At one o'clock the landing was effected, and without much delay. Although everybody seemed to be there and the preparations were elaborate, the party was allowed to reach the quarters assigned expeditiously, conveyed in jiurickshaws, which is described as resembling an invalid chair, propelled by one man in the rear and two in front. The distance from the wharf to the normal school building assigned the General was half a mile. The entire route was decorated with flags of both nations.

A deputation representing the foreign residents of the town first received audience. Their address read thus:

General U. S. Grant—You have been so feted in other lands during your two years' tour that now, as you cross the threshold of this ancient Empire, which in twenty-five years has attempted to revolutionize the traditions of twenty-five centuries, we, representing the foreign community of Nagasaki, are sensible that any welcome we can offer you will appear but a poor one compared with the receptions you have met with from the larger and more wealthy ports in China. Be assured, however, that no more genuine feelings of respect and admiration exist in any community than those which are felt towards you by the foreign residents in Nagasaki, and which prompt us to offer you our sincere and hearty welcome to Japan. We feel much gratified by your visit. We wish you a pleasant journey through this Empire and a safe return to the country of your birth to enjoy the reward of your brave deeds and successful government. We have the honor to be, with much respect, your obedient servants.

To this the General replied as follows:

GENTLEMEN—It is very gratifying to me to have this welcome from the foreign residents of Nagasaki on the occasion of my landing in Japan. It has long been my wish to visit Japan, a nation which has always interested me and for whose efforts to advance in all the benefits of our civilization the American people have had so much sympathy. I hope that all foreign nations will continue to give Japan sympathy and encouragement. I hope also that she will long enjoy peace and especially be at peace with her neighbors. This will be a blessing to her as well as to the rest of the world. I thank you very much for your kind words of welcome, which show not alone your good feeling to me, but what I value more—your good feeling to my country."

The American Minister at Japan, Judge Bingham, arrived in the evening. He reported cholera along the seaboard, so it was decided not to stop between Nagasaki and Yokohama. Two days later the Governor of the Province gave a grand dinner, at the close of which the following address was presented to General Grant:

GENERAL GRANT AND GENTLEMEN—After a two years' tour through many lands Nagasaki has been honored by a visit from the ex-President of the United States. Nagasaki is situated on the western shore of this Empire, and how fortunate it is that I, in my official capacity as Governor of Nagasaki, can greet and welcome you, sir, as you land for the first time on the soil of Japan. Many years ago, honored sir, I learned to appreciate your great services, and during a visit to the United States I was filled with an ardent desire to learn more of your illustrious deeds. You were then the President of the United States, and little then did I anticipate that I should be the first Governor to receive you in Japan. Words cannot express my feelings. Nagasaki is so far from the seat of government that I fear you cannot have matters arranged to your satisfaction. It is my earnest wish that you and Mrs. Grant may safely travel through Japan and enjoy the visit.

This address was spoken in Japanese. At its close an interpreter, who stood behind His Excellency during its delivery, advanced and read the above translation. When the Governor finished General Grant arose and said:

YOUR EXCELLENCY, LADIES AND GENTLEMEN—You have here to-night several Americans who have the talent of speech, and who could make an eloquent response to the address in which my health is proposed. I have no such gift, and I never lamented its absence more than now, when there is so much that I want to say about your country, your people and your progress. I have not been an inattentive observer of that progress, and in America we have been favored with accounts of it from my distinguished friend, whom you all know as the friend of Japan, and whom it was my privilege to send as Minister—I mean Judge Bingham. The spirit which has actuated the mission of Judge Bingham—the spirit of sympathy, support and conciliation—not only expressed my own sentiments, but those of America. America has much to gain in the East—no nation has greater interests—but America has nothing to gain except what comes from the cheerful acquiescence of the Eastern people and insures them as much benefit as it does us. I should be ashamed of my country if its relations with other nations, and especially with these ancient and most interesting empires in the East, were based upon any other idea. We have rejoiced over your progress. We have watched you step by step. We have followed the unfolding of your old civilization and its absorbing the new. You have had our profound sympathy in that work, our sympathy in the troubles which came with it, and our friendship. I hope it may continue—that it may long continue. As I have said: America has great interests in the East. She is your next neighbor. She is more affected by the Eastern populations than any other Power. She can never be insensible to what is doing here. Whatever her influence may be, I am proud to think that it has always been exerted in behalf of justice and kindness. No nation needs from the outside Powers justice and kindness more than Japan, because the work that has made such marvellous progress in the past few years is a work in which we are deeply concerned, in the success of which we see a new era in civilization and which we should encourage. I do not know, gentlemen, that I can say anything more than this in response to the kind words of the Governor. Judge Bingham can speak with much more eloquence and much more authority as our Minister. But I could not allow the occasion to pass without saying how deeply I sympathized with Japan in her efforts to advance, and how much those efforts were appreciated in America. In that spirit I ask you to unite with me in a sentiment:—"The prosperity and the independence of Japan."

There was not very much to detain a traveler at Nagasaki. It is a town of about thirty thousand inhabitants, situate on a peninsula of the island of Kin Sin. He left there in time for the "Richmond" to reach Yokohama July 3d. It was a lovely Summer day when she came to anchor in the bay of the same name as the city. The *Herald* correspondent writing of this reception some days later, says:

". There were men-of-war of various nations in the harbor, and as the exact hour of the General's coming was known, everybody was on the lookout. At ten o'clock our Japanese convoy passed ahead and entered the harbor. At half-past ten the "Richmond" steamed slowly in, followed by the Ashuelot. As soon as the Monongahela made out our flag, and especially the flag at the fore, which denoted the General's presence, her guns rolled out a salute. For a half hour the bay rang with the roar of cannon and was clouded with smoke. The "Richmond" fired a salute to the flag of Japan. The Japanese vessels, the French, the Russian, all fired gun after gun. Then came the official visits. Admiral Patterson and staff, the admirals and commanding officers of other fleets, Consul General Van Buren, officers of the Japanese navy, blazing in uniform; the officers of the "Richmond" were all in full uniform and for an hour the deck of the flagship was a blaze of color and decoration.

It was noon when the landing occurred. An hour later and a special train was bearing the General and his party swiftly over the eighteen miles which stretch between Yokohama and Tokio. The former is the commercial capital, the latter the political capital. All along the route there were evidences of commotion and expectancy, but the train did not halt until its destination was reached. The country passed through had every sign of high cultivation and great prosperity. Hardly had the General alighted from the coach before a committee of citizens advanced to address him, as follows:

Sir—On behalf of the people of Tokio we beg to congratulate you on your safe arrival. How you crushed a rebellion and afterwards ruled a nation in peace and righteousness is known over the whole world, and there is not a man in Japan who does not admire your high character and illustrious career. Although the great Pacific Ocean stretches for thousands of miles between your country and ours your people are our next neighbors in the East, and, as it was chiefly through your initiative that we entered upon those relations and that commerce with foreigners which have now attained such a flourishing condition, our countrymen have always cherished a good feeling for your people and look upon them more than any other foreign nation as their true friends. Moreover, it was during the happy times of your Presidency that the two countries became more closely acquainted and connected, and almost every improvement that has been made in our country may be traced to the example and lessons received from yours. For years past not only our Minister, but any one of our countrymen who went to your country, was received with hospitality and courtesy. It is therefore impossible that our countrymen should now forbear from giving expression to their gratification and gratitude.

Your visit to our shores is one of those rare events that happen once in a thousand years. The citizens of Tokio consider it a great honor that they have been afforded the opportunity of receiving you as their guest, and they cherish the hope that this event will still more cement the friendship between the two nations in the future. We now offer you a hearty and respectful welcome.

General Grant responded:

GENTLEMEN—I am very much obliged for this kind reception, and especially for your address. It affords me great pleasure to visit Tokio. I have been some days in Japan, having seen several points of interest in the interior and on the inland sea. I have been gratified to witness the prosperity and advancement of which I had heard so much, and in which my countrymen have taken so deep an interest. I am pleased to hear your kind expressions toward the United States. We have no sentiment there that is not friendly to Japan, that does not wish her prosperity and independence, and a continuance on her part of her noble policy. The knowledge that your country is prosperous and advancing is most gratifying to the people of the United States. It is my sincere wish that this friendship may never be broken. For this kind welcome to the capitol of Japan I am again very much obliged.

The Emperor's private carriage then whirled him away to the summer palace, which had been prepared for his especial occupancy. With an eye to fitness and *eclat* it was arranged that the reception of the General by the Emperor should occur on the next day, (July 4). Accordingly, the next day a drive was taken through the aristocratic part of the city, from General Grant's palace to the royal palace. Earthquakes are not unfrequent in that country, and this accounts probably, for the fact that the architecture of

Tokio is not at all imposing. Even the palace of the Emperor is a low, plain structure. "The home of the Emperor," writes one of the party, "was as simple as that of a country gentleman at home. We have many country gentlemen with felicitous investments in petroleum and silver who would disdain the home of a prince who claims direct descent from heaven, and whose line extends far beyond the Christian era. What marked the house was its simplicity and taste."

The same writer gives an interesting description of the Japanese Cabinet, as it accompanied the Emperor on the occasion of his formal reception of General Grant, and of the Emperor himself, and the Empress. He writes:

"The Japanese Cabinet is a famous body, and tested by laws of physiognomy would compare with that of any Cabinet I have seen. The Prime Minister is a striking character. He is small, slender, with an almost girl-like figure, delicate, clean cut, winning features, a face that might be that of a boy of twenty or a man of fifty. The Prime Minister reminded me of Alexander H. Stephens in his frail, slender frame, but it bloomed with health and lacked the sad, pathetic lines which tell of the years of suffering which Stephens has endured. The other Ministers looked like strong, able men. Iwakura has a striking face, with lines showing firmness and decision, and you saw the scar which marked the attempt of the assassin to cut him down and slay him, as Okubo, the greatest of Japanese statesmen was slain not many months ago. That assassination made as deep an impression in Japan as the killing of Lincoln did in America.

"We walked along a short passage and entered another room, at the father end of which were standing the Emperor and the Empress. Two ladies in waiting were near them. in a sitting, what appeared to be a crouching attitude. Two other princesses were standing. These were the only occupants of the room. Our party slowly advanced, the Japanese making a profound obeisance, bending the head almost to a right angle with the body. The royal princes formed in line near the Emperor, along with the princesses. The Emperor stood quite motionless, apparently unobservant, or unconscious of the homage that was paid him. He is a young man with a slender figure, taller than the average Japanese and of about the middle height, according to our ideas. He has a striking face, with mouth and lips that remind you something of the traditional mouth of the Hapsburg family. The forehead is full and narrow, the hair and the light mustasche and beard intensely black. The color of the hair darkens what otherwise might pass for a swarthy countenance at home. The face expressed no feeling whatever, and but for the dark, glowing eye, which was bent full upon the General, you might have taken the imperial group for statutes. The Empress at his side, wore the Japanese costume, rich and plain. Her face was very white and her form slender and almost childlike. Her hair was combed plainly and braided with a gold arrow. The Emperor and Empress have agreeable faces, the Emperor especially showing firmness and kindness. The solemn etiquette that pervaded the audience chamber was peculiar, and might appear strange to those familiar with the stately but cordial manners of a European Court. But one must remember that the Emperor holds so high and so sacred a place in the traditions, the religion and the political system of Japan, that even the ceremony of to-day is so far in advance of anything of the kind ever known in

Japan, that it might be called a revolution. The Emperor cordially shook hands with the General. Such an incident was never known in the history of Japanese Majesty."

The address and replies of the occasion were remarkable in that the Empress and Mrs. Grant took part in the interchange of formal greetings. The advocates of equal rights for women, should elect Her Imperial Majesty and her more than royal sister honorable members of their societies.

The address to General Grant was as follows:

"Your name has been known to us for a long time, and we are highly gratified to see you. While holding the high office of President of the United States, you extended to our countrymen especial kindness and courtesy. When our Ambassador, Iwakura, visited the United States he received the greatest kindness from you. The kindness thus shown by you has always been remembered by us. In your travels around the world you have reached this country, and our people of all classes feel gratified and happy to receive you. We trust that during your sojourn in our country you may find much to enjoy. It gives me sincere pleasure to receive you, and we are especially gratified that we have been able to do so on the anniversary of American Independence. We congratulate you, also, on the occasion."

This address was read in English. At its close General Grant said:

YOUR MAJESTY—I am very grateful for the welcome you accord me here to day, and for the great kindness with which I have been received, ever since I came to Japan, by your government and your people. I recognize in this a feeling of friendship toward my country. I can assure you that this feeling is reciprocated by the United States;

that our people, without regard to party, take the deepest interest in all that concerns Japan, and have the warmest wishes for her welfare. I am happy to be able to express that sentiment. America is your next neighbor, and will always give Japan sympathy and support in her efforts to advance. I again thank your Majesty for your hospitality, and wish you a long and happy reign, and for your people prosperity and independence."

The Empress then addressed Mrs. Grant thus:

"I congratulate you upon your safe arrival after your long journey. I presume you have seen very many interesting places. I fear you will find many things uncomfortable here, because the customs of the country are so different from other countries. I hope you will prolong your stay in Japan and that the present warm days may occasion you no inconvenience."

Mrs. Grant replied:

"I thank you very much. I have visited many countries and have seen many beautiful places, but I have seen none so beautiful or so charming as Japan."

This was enough for one day, it might be thought, but Independence Day comes only once a year, and such an occasion as that would never repeat itself. In the evening the Americans had a banquet and more speeches. What Minister Bingham and General Grant said are worthy of preservation. The former said:

"In common with all Americans we are not unmindful that in the supreme moment of our national trials, when our heavens were filled with darkness and our habitations were filled with dead, you stood with our defenders in the forefront of the conflict and with them amid the consuming fires of battle achieved the victory which brought deliverence to our imperrilled country. To found a great commonwealth or to save from overthrow a great commonwealth already founded is considered to be the greatest of human achievements. If it was not your good fortune to aid Washington, first of Americans and foremost of men, and his peerless associates in founding the Republic; it was given to you above all others to aid in the no less honorable work of saving the Republic from overthrow." Mr. Bingham continued his speech, saying :—" Now that the sickle has fallen from the pale hand of Death on the field of mortal combat, and the places which but yesterday were blackened and blasted by war have grown green and beautiful under the hand of peaceful toil ; now that the Republic, one and undivided, is covered with the greatness of justice, protecting each by the combined power of all—men of every land and every tongue—the world, appreciating the fact that your civic and military services largely contributed to these results, so essential not only to the interests of our own country, but to the interests of the human race, have accorded to you such honors as never before within the range of authentic history have been given to a living, untitled and unofficial person. I may venture to say that this grateful recognition of your services will not be limited to the present generation or the present age, but will continue through all the ages. In conclusion I beg leave again to bid you welcome to Japan, and to express the wish that in health and prosperity you may return to your native land, the land which we all love so well."

In response General Grant said:

LADIES AND GENTLEMEN—I am unable to answer the eloquent speech of Judge Bingham, as it is in so many senses personal to myself. I can only thank him for his too flattering allusions to me personally and the duty devolving on me during the late war. We had a great war. We had a trial that summoned forth the energies and patriotism of all our people—in the army alone over a million. In awarding credit for the success that crowned those efforts there is not one in that million, not one among the living or the dead, who did not do his share as I did mine, and who does not deserve as much credit. It fell to my lot to command the armies. There were many others who could have commanded the armies better. But I did my best, and we all did our best, and in the fact that it was a struggle on the part of the people for the Union, for the country, for a country for themselves and their children, we have the best assurances of peace and the best reason for gratification over the result. We are strong and free because the people made us so. I trust we may long continue so. I think we have no issues, no questions that need give us embarrassment. I look forward to peace, to generations of peace, and with peace prosperity. I never felt more confident of the future of our country. It is a great country—a great blessing to us—and we cannot be too proud of it, too zealous for its honor, too anxious to develop its resources, and make it not only a home for our children, but for the worthy people of other lands. I am glad to meet you here, and I trust that your labors will be prosperous, and that you will return home in health and happiness. I trust we may all meet again at home and be able to celebrate our Fourth of July as pleasantly as we do tonigh

A few days later there was a Grand Military parade, the General's pet aversion. The Emperor takes a great interest in his army. It is necessary to maintain peace at home. The damios are kept in wholesome awe. It may

JAPAN—THE LOVERS' ROCK.

JAPAN—JAPANESE ROW-BOAT.

as well be stated here that a revolution of the utmost importance changed Japan, a few years ago, from an aggregation of independent and hostile barons and their respective retainers into a homogenous people with a national soverenity. The benefits of the change are very great, but "bayonet rule" is sometimes necessary to maintain the peace.

The Emperor subsequently sought and obtained an interview with General Grant in regard to the Loochoo questions, already referred to. The latter did not commit himself. He counseled a pacific settlement. and urged it strongly. That was about all he could do. It is a very old and complicated dispute, dating back more than a thousand years. It is not likely that the General had any conception of its antiquity and complications, when he consented to inform himself upon it, although he could hardly have done less than to have promised that much. The reader shall be spared the details. It is enough to know that the Loochoo Islands, thirty-six in number, were first captured by Yang-ti, 605, A. D., after a bloody war.

General Grant spent from July 17 to August 19 in visiting the country. He first went to the shrine of Iyeyasu, the founder of the great Tokegausa family, at Nikko, a famous and sacred resort, one hundred miles inland. He also took in Kamakara, the ancient seat of Military Government, and its neighborhood, and the mountain pass of Hakone.

In this connection may be inserted a letter written by General Grant during his stay at Tokio, to a personal friend in this country. It is all the more interesting from the fact that it was not designed for publication:

"We expect to sail on the "City of Tokio," which is to leave here for San Francisco on the 27th of August. We have now been in Japan nearly a month the guests of the nation, and have received the most unbounded hospitalities. Our first stop in the country was at Nagasaki, where we remained a week. It was a continuous ovation while we remained. From Nagasaki we came up through the Inland Sea to Yokohama, anchoring at night, so as to lose no part of the scenery. It is grand beyond description, and strongly in contrast with what we had left in China. In Japan, the country is mountainous, and green and fresh to the summit of the highest hills. In China, so far as the foreigner usually sees it, it is a flat, desert looking dust or mud plain— depending upon whether it is the dry or rainy season—without anything to relieve the eye. The scenery up through the Inland Sea is very grand, and we get as good a view of it as is possible from the deck of a steamer, but we did not land anywhere. The cholera had broken out a few days before our arrival all along the borders of the sea, and was carrying off the people by hundreds. * * * * What I said at Penango about the Chinese question was without previous thought or preparation. I had no idea what the address to me was to be until it was read in the presence of an assembly. The response had to be spontaneous, and now I see nothing in particular to alter or take back. The fact is, the Chinese question is not going to agitate the country long. The Chinese Government are very anxious to keep all their people at home, and, if not interfered with, they will stop emigration."

A pleasant episode was the attempt of General and Mrs. Grant to visit a noted temple in a perfectly private way; it was not long however, before he was recognized and known. The priests were delighted at the honor shown their place of worship, and displayed before them the many sacred things, not usually exposed to secular eyes.

The President's leave-taking of Japan, and at the same time of the entire Old World, was very imposing. The General and Mrs. Grant bid adieu to the Emperor and Empress in the same room in which they were first received, the circumstances being substantially the same. After the hand-shaking, there was a moment's pause, when General Grant took from his pocket and read the following farewell:

"YOUR MAJESTY :—I come to take my leave and to thank you, the officers of your government and the people of Japan for the great hospitality and kindness I have received at the hands of all during my most pleasant visit to this country. I have now been two months in Tokio and the surrounding neighborhood, and two previous weeks in the more southerly part of the country. It affords me great satisfaction to say that during all this stay and all my visiting, I have not witnessed one discourtesy toward myself nor a single unpleasant sight. Everywhere there seems to be the greatest contentment among the people ; and while no signs of great individual wealth exist no absolute poverty is visible. This is in striking and pleasing contrast with almost every other country I have visited. I leave Japan greatly impressed with the possibilities and probabilities of her future. She has a fertile soil, one-half of it not yet cultviated to man's use, great undeveloped mineral rescources, numerous and fine harbors, an extensive seacoast abounding in fish of an almost endless variety, and above all, an industrions, ingenious, contented and frugal population. With all these nothing is wanted to insure great progress except wise direction by the government, peace at home and abroad and non-interference in the internal and domestic affairs of the country by the outside nations. It is the sincere desire of your guest to see Japan realize all possible strength and greatness, to see her as independent of foreign rule or dictation as any Western nation now is, and to see affairs so directed by her as to command the respect of the civilized world. In saying this I believe I reflect the sentiments of the great majority of my countrymen. I now take my leave without expectation of ever again having the opportunity of visiting Japan, but with the assurance that pleasant recollections of my present visit will not vanish while my life lasts. That Your Majesty may long reign over a prosperous and contented people and enjoy every blessing is my sincere prayer."

When General Grant had finished, Mr. Ishibashi, the interpreter, read a Japanese translation. The Emperor bowed, and taking from an attendant a scroll on which was written in Japanese letters his own address, read it as follows:

"Your visit has given us so much satisfaction and pleasure that we can only lament that the time for your departure has come. We regret also that the heat of the season and the presence of the epidemic have prevented several of your proposed visits to different places. In the meantime, however, we have greatly enjoyed the pleasure of frequent interviews with you; and the cordial expressions which you have just addressed to us in taking your leave have given us great additional satisfaction. America and Japan being near neighbors, separated by an ocean only, will become more and more closely connected with each other as time goes on. It is gratifying to feel assured that your visit to our Empire, which enabled us to form very pleasant personal acquaintance with each other, will facilitate and strengthen the friendly relations that have heretofore happily existed between the two countries. And now we cordially wish you a safe and pleasant voyage home, and that you will on your return home find your nation in peace and prosperity, and that you and your family may enjoy long life and happiness."

His Majesty read his speech in a clear, pleasant voice. Mr. Ishibashi at the close also read a translation. Then the Empress, addressing herself to Mrs. Grant, said she rejoiced to see the General and party in Japan, but she was afraid the unusual heat and the pestilence had prevented them from enjoying her visit. Mrs. Grant said that her visit to Japan had more than realized her anticipations; that she had enjoyed every hour of her stay in this most beautiful country, and that she hoped she might have in her American home, at some early day, an opportunity of acknowledging and returning the hospitality she had received in Japan.

The Emperor then addressed Mr. Bingham, our Minister, hoping he was well and expressing his pleasure at seeng him again. Mr. Bingham advanced and said:

"I thank Your Majesty for your kind inquiry. I desire, on behalf of the President of the United States and of the government and people I represent, to express our profound appreciation of the kindness and the honor shown by Your Majesty and your people to our illustrious citizen."

His Majesty expressed his pleasure at the speech of Mr. Bingham, the audience came to an end, and the party drove back to Euriokwan, where they remained until morning, when a special train bore them from the city of Tokio to the "City of Tokio," in waiting at Yokahoma for them. Of this leave-taking Mr. Young writes the following, which can best close this chapter:

"In saying farewell to our Japanese friends; to those who had been our special hosts, General Grant expressed his gratitude and his friendship. But mere words, however warmly spoken, could only give faint expression to the feelings with which we took leave of many of those who had come to the steamer to pay us parting courtesy. These gentlemen were not alone princes—rulers of an Empire, noblemen of rank and lineage, Ministers of a Sovereign whose guests we had been—but friends. And in saying farewell to them we said farewell to so many and so much, to a country where every hour of our stay had a special value, to a civilization which had profoundly impressed us and which awakened new ideas of what Japan had been, of her real place in the world and of what her place might be if stronger nations shared her generosity or justice. We had been strangely won by Japan, and our last view of it was a scene of beauty. Yokohama nestled on her shore, against which the waters of the sea were idly rolling. Her hills were dowered with foliage, and here and there were houses and groves and flagstaffs, sentinels of the outside world which had made this city their encampment. In the far distance, breaking through the clouds, so faint at first that you had to look closely to make sure that you were not deceived by the mists, Fusiyama towered into the blue and bending skies. Around us were men-of-war shimmering in the sunshine, so it seemed, with their multitudinous flags. There was the hurry, the nervous bustle and excitement, the glow of energy and feeling which always mark the last moments of a steamer about to sail. Our naval friends went back to their ships. Our Yokohama friends went off in their tugs, and the last we saw of General Van Buren was a distant and vanishing figure in a state of pantomime, as though he were delivering a Fourth of July oration. I presume he was cheering. Then our Japanese friends took leave, and went on board their steam launch to accompany us a part of our journey. The Japanese man-of-war has her anchor up, slowly steaming, ready to carry us out to sea. The last line that binds us to our anchorage is thrown off, and the hugh steamer moves slowly through the shipping. We pass the "Richmond" near enough to recognize our friends on the quarter deck—the Admiral and his officers. You hear a shrill word of command, and seamen go scampering up the rigging to man the yards. The guns roll out a salute. We pass the "Ashuelot," and her guns take up the iron chorus. We pass the "Monongahela" so close almost that we could converse with Captain Fitzhugh and the gentlemen who are waving us farewell. Her guns thunder good-bye, and over the bay the smoke floats in waves—floats on towards Fusiyama. We hear the cheers from the "Ranger." Very soon all that we see of our vessels are faint and distant phantoms, and all that we see of Yokohama is a line of gray and green. We are fast speeding on toward California. For an hour or so, the Japanese man-of-war, the same which met us at Nagasaki and came with us through the Inland Sea, keeps us company. The Japanese Cabinet are on board. We see the smoke break from her ports and we hurry to the side of the vessel to say farewell—farewell to so many friends, so many friends kind and true. This is farewell at last, our final token of good will from Japan. The man-of-war fires twenty-one guns. The Japanese sailors swarm on the rigging and give hearty cheers. Out steamer answers by blowing her steam whistle. The man-of-war turns slowly around and steams back to Yokohama. Very soon she also becomes a phantom, vanishing over the horizon. Then, gathering herself like one who knows of a long and stern task to do, our steamer breasts the sea with an earnest will—for California and for home."

CHAPTER XXIV.

THE PACIFIC VOYAGE.

THE RETURN TO AMERICA—ACROSS THE PACIFIC—HOW THE GENERAL SPENT HIS TIME ON SHIPBOARD — STORIES AND REMINISCENCES — HIS OPINION OF THE BATTLE OF WATERLOO—HIS DETESTATION OF NAPOLEON—CORRECTIONS OF SOME FOOLISH STORIES ABOUT GENERAL GRANT—HIS CONVERSATION WITH THE VICEROY OF TIENTSIN—HIS MEETING WITH BAYARD TAYLOR IN BERLIN—AN ENGLISH ESTIMATE OF GRANT.

The time had now come for General Grant to return to the United States. His journeyings had already been extended by the unexpected and urgent hospitality which he had everywhere met, far beyond the limits originally set by him; and he was growing anxious to return, like the older Ulysses after his wanderings, to his own country.

Sailing from Philadelphia eastward, two and a half years before, he had crossed the Atlantic to England; and he was to complete the circumnavigation of the globe by again sailing eastward, across the Pacific, to his native shores.

The vessel in which he made his last and longest voyage was the "Tokio," a magnificent steamship of the Pacific Mail Line. They left Yokohama on the 3d of September. The weather almost always pleasant on those mild Pacific seas, made the trip a thoroughly enjoyable one, and very restful to the General after the fatigues of traveling, visiting and sight-seeing in China and Japan. The long days were spent in smoking and walking upon deck, and in pleasant conversations with his companions. The General's conversational and other personal qualities, which had abundant opportunity for display on his home voyage, are thus spoken of by Mr. Young, the correspondent of the New York *Herald:*

"When the General is in the mood, or when some subject arises which interests him, he is not only a good, but a remarkably good, talker. His manner is clear and terse. He narrates a story as clearly as he would demonstrate a problem in geometry. His mind is accurate and perspicacious. He has no resentments, and this was a surprising feature, remembering the battles, civil and military, in which he has been engaged. I have heard him refer to most of the men, civil and military, who have flourished with him, and there is only one about whom I have seen him show feeling. But it was feeling like that of the farmer in the school-book who saw the viper which he had warmed to life about to sting him. I had known General Grant fairly well before I became the companion of his travels, and had formed my own opinion of his services and character. A closer relation strengthens that opinion. The impression that the General makes upon you is that he has immense resources in reserve. He has in eminent degree that 'two o'clock in the morning courage' which Napoleon said he alone possessed among his marshals and generals. You are also impressed with his good feeling and magnanimity in speaking of comrades and rivals in the war. In some cases—especially in the cases of Sherman and Sheridan, MacPherson and Lincoln—it becomes an enthusiasm quite beautiful to witness. Cadet days are a favorite theme of conversation, and after cadet life the events of the war.

The General read a great deal on the home voyage, and commented freely on the books that interested him. The account of the battle of Waterloo, in Victor Hugo's "Les Misérables," particularly pleased him; and he remarked that it was one of the best descriptions of a battle he had ever read. He said that he agreed with Hugo in one thing about the battle,—that it seemed that the time had come for Napoleon to fall; that the battle was a perfect one so far as any military genius could devise it, and there could be no criticism made upon Napoleon's manner of planning it and fighting it. He had a great detestation of the character of Napoleon, whom he regarded as one of the most selfish men in history. "I think if Napoleon," General Grant said on one occasion, "had been a thoroughly unselfish man, a patriot, and one who cared about his country, not about the advancement of his family and personal power, he would have been, without comparison, the greatest man in history; but as it turned out he was one of the worst. I never had any sympathy with him, nor respect for his achievements, although, of course, I cannot but wonder at his marvelous genius." The General's opinion of the character of Napoleon is further shown by an incident that occurred on the French ship going to Hong Kong. One of the young ladies asked General Grant to write in a book called "Questions and Answers," a sort of young ladies' album much in vogue. One of the questions was, "Which two characters in history do you dislike most?" He wrote: "Napoleon and Robespierre."

A great many very interesting reminiscences of General Grant's travels, with incidents illustrating his character and the impressions of others concerning him, are worth preserving, and some of them may be not inappropriately given here.

Of the General's qualities as a traveler, Mr. Young says: "General Grant is a severe traveler: one of extraordinary endurance. Always prompt and anxious to get on, he saw things very rapidly, and never was more satisfied than when he could travel all night and see sights all day. He seemed to enjoy sea life more than anything else." Though he everywhere met with grand displays in his honor, his own desire was to travel as quietly and unostentatiously as possible. According to Mr. Young, he "Declines all honors and attentions, so far as he can do so without rudeness, and is especially indifferent to the parade and etiquette by which his journey is surrounded. He has uniformly declined every attention of an official character, except those whose non-acceptance would have been misconstrued. When he arrives at a port his habit is to go ashore with his wife and son, see what is to be seen, and drift about from palace to picture gallery like any other wandering, studious American doing Europe. Sometimes the officials are too prompt for him; but generally, unless they call by appointment, they find the General absent."

There have been so many mis-statements and perversions of fact regarding General Grant's foreign travels, by reckless journals, which have sought to make political or sensational capital of such reports, that, ridiculous as some of these statements are, it is perhaps worth while to note here their falsity. We gladly quote from the *Herald* correspondent upon this point:

"General Grant travels with a princely retinue; he is enabled to do so because the men who fattened on the corruptions of his administration gave him a share of their plunder. He went to the Hotel Bristol in Paris. He took the Prince of Wales's apartments. He never asks the cost of his rooms at hotels, but throws money about with a lavish hand. These are the statements which one reads here in the columns of an American journal. The truth is that General Grant travels not like a prince, but as a private citizen. He has one servant and a courier. He never was in the Prince of Wales's apartments in the Hotel Bristol in his life. His courier arranges for his hotel accommodations, as couriers always do, and the one who does this office for the General takes pains to make as good bargains for his master as possible. So far from General Grant being a rich man, I think I am not breaking confidence when I say that the duration of his trip will depend altogether upon his income, and his income depends altogether upon the proceeds of his investment of the money presented to him at the close of the war. The Presidency yielded him nothing in the way of capital, and he has not now a dollar that came to him as an official. By this I mean that the money paid General Grant as a soldier and as a President was spent by him in supporting the dignity of his office. Everybody knows how much money was given him at the close of the war. As this was all well invested and has grown, you may estimate the fortune of the General and about how long that fortune would enable him to travel like a prince or a Tammany exile over Europe. There are many people at home who do not like General Grant, who quarrel with his politics and think his administration a calamity. That is a matter of opinion. But his fame as a soldier is dear to every patriotic American, and I am glad of the opportunity of brushing away one or two of the cobwebs of slander which I see growing over it."

A great deal of newspaper comment has been made upon a conversation which took place while General Grant was in China, between him and the Viceroy of Tientsin, in which the General departed slightly from his uniform habit while abroad, of refusing to talk upon American politics. We give the conversation here, as reported by the *Herald* correspondent:

In answer to some remarks of the Viceroy, who expressed the hope that the General would be re-elected to a third term for the Presidency, General Grant said:

Your Excellency is very kind, but there could be no wish more distasteful to me than what you express. I have held the office of President as long as it has ever been held by any man. There are others who have risen to great distinction at home and who have earned the honor who are worthy, and to them it belongs, not to me. I have no claims to the office. It is a place distasteful to me, a place of hardship and responsibilities. When I was a younger man these hardships were severe and never agreeable. They would be worse now.

THE VICEROY—But you are a young man and your experience would be of value.

GENERAL GRANT—No man who knows what the Presidency imposes would care to see a friend in the office. I have had my share of it—have had all the honors that can be or should be given to any citizen, and there are many able and distinguished men who have earned the office. To one of them it should be given.

The Viceroy smiling, said that the General showed himself to be what he always heard—a modest man—and he still hoped, for the good relations between China and America alone, that he would be again President. The Viceroy said he had read in some Chinese papers translations from the American papers about the great reception that was awaiting the General in California, and supposed he would time his arrival so as to meet it.

GENERAL GRANT—I would much rather time my arrival so as to avoid it. But most of these paragraphs are exaggerations and others are written in an unfriendly spirit. It is possible some personal friends may come to meet me from the East—a half dozen perhaps—who will take the occasion to run over to California. I have a good many friends on the Pacific coast, whom I will be glad to see. But my time of return is unknown, and the stories that have crept into the Chinese papers about monster excursions are exaggerations.

General Grant's ready tact, as well as his genuine kindness of heart and the readiness with which he makes friends of those with whom he is brought in contact, even when there are strong prepossessions against him, are well illustrated in Mr. Young's story of the meeting between the General and Bayard Taylor at Berlin.

"On my return to Berlin," says Mr. Young, "Bayard Taylor informed me that General Grant was coming, and together we went down the road to meet him, about sixty miles. Taylor had never met Grant and was quite nervous, I remember, about seeing him. He had been a supporter of Mr. Greeley. Naturally, as an editor of the *Tribune*, he had shared in the conservative Republican dislike of General Grant and seemed anxious about the meeting. I had known Taylor intimately for years. He was essentially a high strung gentleman and I was afraid there might be some coolness in Grant's reception in Berlin, and that Grant might attribute it to Taylor's personal political affinities, but remember, also, that at his first meeting with the General he quite captivated Taylor. When we came to the station at Stendahl and General Grant's car arrived, I introduced the Minister to him. The General presented him to Mrs. Grant, and, turning around, said: "By the way, Mrs Grant, you remember that when we were first married I read aloud to you Mr. Taylor's book, 'Views Afoot,' during the evening?" "Yes," said Mrs. Grant, "what a charming book it was, and I am so glad to meet the author." The General could not have said anything more calculated to win the respect of Taylor than this unintended little com pliment. General Grant remained in Berlin a week, and I remember Taylor saying to me, the last day of the visit, how delighted he was at having met General Grant; how the General's character had won upon him, and that he could never have for him anything but lasting esteem; that the Grant of politics and of strife had passed away, and in his place had come a personal friend."

There is something very curious in the English estimates of General Grant. One of them is thus given in a leading London journal:

"On the whole, Grant may be described as about the one great gun America has turned out since Washington— Lincoln, perhaps, and certainly Longfellow, excepted. He is, moreover, a truer exemplification of his country's genius than either of those eminent men. For the typical Yankee is Jack of all Trades, and has proved an old proverb false by being good at many things. Grant for instance, has been tanner, farmer, banker, soldier, politician. Among the few men who can manage to make him talk is Lord Napier of Magdala. Grant's delight with Gibralter, of which Lord Napier is Governor, was unbounded. He liked everything and man about it, from "His Excellency," downward, and said that no spot in the British Empire had made him understand better the secret of England's power. The silent warrior, one sees, can occasionally pay a stately and graceful compliment. Grant likes us, on the whole, and is reasonably proud of his Scotch origin. If the Alabama business never ended in a tragic way—which it well might have—the praise is probably due to him."

But we have wandered far from the "Tokio" and her distinguished passenger, of whom we have been giving these rambling reminiscences. Day by day the vessel pursued her stately course, and nearer and nearer grew the coast of California. On the morning of September 20th the shore was in sight; and early in the afternoon the vessel entered the Golden Gate, where a signal gun announced her presence to the expectant people of San Francisco, and, reverberated on the electric wire, to a waiting nation.

CHAPTER XXV.

HOME AGAIN.

ARRIVAL AT SAN FRANCISCO—CHANGE IN THE FEELINGS OF THE AMERICAN PEOPLE TOWARD GRANT—SOME OF THE CAUSES—A GRAND RECEPTION—SCENE IN SAN FRANCISCO HARBOR—THE LANDING—A MAGNIFICIENT DISPLAY—SOME OF THE GENERAL'S SPEECHES IN SAN FRANCISCO—UP THE COAST—RECEPTION IN OREGON—RETURN TO SAN FRANCISCO—SACRAMENTO AND THE YO SEMITE—EASTWARD BOUND—REMARKS TO THE NEVADA MINERS—ARRIVAL AT GALENA.

Between the time when General Grant left his native shores, in May, 1877, and his return, in September, 1879, a great and surprising change had taken place in the feelings of the people of his untry toward him. His departure at Philadelphia, while it was witnessed by a good many of his personal and official friends, who were sincere and hearty in their adieus and well-wishes, was comparatively a tame and undemonstrative affair, and attracted no special attention from the country at large. Probably not half a dozen persons were even aware that he had gone, out of every hundred—perhaps thousand—who are familiar with every detail of his return. His departure was chronicled briefly and casually by the press, with other events of the day; many of them far more conspicuously. His arrival is beyond comparison the one leading and absorbing topic of the time. For weeks his name has been upon every tongue, and in the columns of every newspaper in the land. His departure was an ordinary and commonplace affair; his return is the occasion of a grand and unparalleled national ovation. He went away a simple and quiet citizen, almost as any other citizen might have done; he returns a hero and a conqueror.

Without going into a discussion of the causes of this remarkable change in public sentiment, which is not within the range of these chronicles, it may be proper to point out hastily the direction in which those causes are most likely to be found. The consideration which the General has received abroad, is undoubtedly an important factor in the matter. It does not make the General a greater man, that he has been feted and lionized by the whole world, but his countrymen are proud of his reception abroad, and proud of the way in which he has borne himself; and their pride naturally takes the form of gratitude and admiration for the man who has conferred so much credit upon American character.

Political changes have doubtless much to do with it, though these it is not in the scope of this work to discuss, further than to recall the fact that the General's departure from the United States was just at the beginning of a new Administration, when public attention was absorbed by the peculiar difficulties and complications of the time. General Grant had just quitted office; his eight years' Administration had closed quietly and successfully; and there was nothing connected with it likely to be made the subject of after-inquiry or examination. The old era had closed, and a new era had arrived with new responsibilities and new questions pressing for solution. Though a Republican President had been inaugurated, and was performing the functions of the actual and legal executive of the government, there was a rival claimant backed by a powerful and determined party; and the time was one of political uncertainty and anxiety. Grant had attained the respectable but inconsequential position of an ex-President; and though deep down in the hearts of the people there were still the ardent sentiments of love and gratitude for the great hero of the war and the preserver of his country, yet for the time more superficial and transitory feelings rushed to the surface, and the movements and purposes of General Grant were by the mass of people unknown and unnoticed.

But whatever doubts and misgivings the General may have had at any time concerning his hold upon the hearts of the American people, must have been quickly and entirely dispelled on his arrival on our shores. He found the people of the Pacific Coast not only, but of the entire country, waiting to receive him and to welcome his return to his native land. The reception at San Francisco was in all respects the most magnificent popular demonstration ever known on the Pacific Coast; and the grandest of its kind that had ever occurred in this country. For weeks before the arrival of the "Tokio," the expected visit was the one absorbing topic of conversation. A committee was appointed for carrying out the formal part of the arrangements, and their management was an admirable blending of prodigality and discretion. At three o'clock on the afternoon of September 20th, after several days of constant expectation, a signal bell announced that the "Tokio" was in sight; and in a few minutes the wharves of the Pacific Mail Company were crowded with thousands of people, all eager to catch the first glimpse of the incoming vessel. A steamer containing the reception committee and some of General Grant's intimate personal friends, as also his youngest son, at once put out to sea to meet the "Tokio," followed by an immense fleet of steamers, yachts, and vessels of all descriptions. There was a brief exchange of salutations on the deck of the "Tokio," and then the fleet turned about and accompanied the steamer on her way into the harbor. It seemed as though the whole population of the city, men, women and children, had sought positions from which a view of the naval pageant could be obtained. Every eminence commanding the channel was black with the assembled thousands, as the steamers and yachts, gay with bunting, moved down the channel. From every flagstaff in the city flags were flying, and the shipping along the city front was brilliantly decked with ensigns, and festooned with flags and streamers. The impatient crowds that covered the hill-tops stood straining their eyes to catch the first glimpse of the "Tokio." A hundred times the cry was raised, "There she comes!" as chance arrivals came in view between the heads. It was half-past 5 o'clock when a puff of white smoke from seaward, followed by the booming of a heavy gun, announced that the steamer was near at hand. Another and another followed in rapid succession. Fort Point next joined in cannonade firing with both casemate and barbette guns, and the battery at Lime Point added its thunders to the voice of welcome. In a few moments the entrance to the harbor was veiled in wreathes of smoke, and, as the batteries of Angel Island, Black Point and Alcatraz opened fire in succession, the whole channel was soon shrouded in clouds from their rapid discharges. For some time the position of the approaching ships could not be discerned, but shortly before 6 o'clock outlines of the huge hull of the "City of Tokio" loomed through the obscurity of the smoke, and the rapidly approaching shades of evening were lit up by flashes of guns, and in a few moments she glided into full view, surrounded by a fleet of steamers and tugs gay with flags and crowded with guests, while the yacht squadron brought up the rear festooned from deck to truck with brilliant bunting. Cheer after cheer burst from the assembled thousands, as the vessels slowly rounded Telegraph Hill, and, taken up by the crowd on the wharves, rolled around the city front. Hats and handkerchiefs were waved in the air. The United States steamer, "Monterey," lying in the stream, added the roar of her guns to the general welcome, and the screaming of hundreds of steam whistles announced that the "City of Tokio" had reached her anchorage.

General Grant and party were now transferred from the deck of the "Tokio" to the steam ferry-boat "Oakland," which proceeded to her wharf. The vicinity was literally jammed with a vast and enthusiastic crowd of people, as the boat reached the landing; and while the band struck up "Home Again," and amid the roars of applause from the waiting crowd outside, who realized that the moment had arrived, General Grant stepped once more upon the shore of his native land.

After an address of welcome by the Mayor of San Francisco, and a brief reply by General Grant, a procession was formed to escort him to his stopping place at the Palace Hotel. As the carriage containing General Grant made its appearance, cheer after cheer went up from thousands of throats, while the surging crowd pressed forward and swayed from side to side in efforts to obtain a passing glance of the familiar lineaments of the Great Captain. The procession started amid the most tremendous cheers of the crowd, discharges of cannon, ringing of bells and screaming of whistles. Bonfires blazed at the street corners, illuminations lit up every window, and the glare of Roman candles and electric lights made the broad thoroughfare bright as day. Under a continuous archway of flags, banners, and festooned draperies, the procession moved along its way, while cheer after cheer rolled along the line of march, and almost drowned the martial strains of the numerous bands. It was ten o'clock before the General's carriage reached the Palace Hotel, where it passed under a magnificent arch, forty feet in hight, blazoned with the National colors, and bearing the inscription, "Welcome to Grant." Leaving his carriage, he made his way with the utmost difficulty through the crowd, and retired to his apartments.

Soon, in response to repeated calls, he appeared on the balcony of the fourth floor, and bowed to the shouting crowd, immediately retiring. Still the enthusiastic populace thronged the court and refused to leave. Presently the General re-appeared, and was again greeted with a succession of cheers. When the noise subsided, he addressed them as follows:

"FELLOW-CITIZENS OF SAN FRANCISCO: After twenty-five years' absence, I am glad to meet you, and assure you of my cordial thanks for the kind greeting you have given me. I shall stay in your city long enough to greet you more fully."

The General then withdrew, amid prolonged and tremendous cheering, and the crowd at length reluctantly scattered.

The greeting which was extended to General Grant on the occasion of his first arrival in San Francisco was but the prelude to the grand and continous ovation which was accorded him during his entire stay in the city, and indeed, on the Pacific Coast. It is not our purpose to follow the details of his visit there, further than to barely enumerate its principal incidents; our narrative having to do more particularly with the General's foreign travels, and dwelling upon the San Francisco ovation because it was the occasion of his first return to his native land. There were a great many other noticeable features of the General's stay in that city—parades, receptions, banquets, etc., some of them rivalling the magnificence of the most splendid Courts which he had visited abroad. Several excellent short speeches were made by General Grant in San Francisco, the most noticeable of which is the one made to the ex-Confederate soldiers who had invited him to be present at their meeting at the City Hall. It was as follows:

"GENTLEMEN: It has afforded me great satisfaction and pleasure to observe the very cordial reception I have received here, and especially the welcome coming from the gentlemen you represented. If you had traveled around the world as I have, for several years past, you would appreciate, like me, the value of our common country more completely than any man can who stays at home. You would be everywhere gratified to see that we are recognized by all the nations of the earth in a higher light than our own people imagine. Abroad our resources are considered unlimited. When one gets to see the nations of the world, he begins to appreciate the inestimable value of our broad acres and the great energy of our people that is forever upbuilding in State, city and town. It affords me very great satisfaction and pleasure to receive the gentlemen who were long ago, opposed to us, and I hope if this country ever sees another war we shall all be together, under one flag, fighting a common enemy."

At the soldiers' and sailors' reunion, where both the Federal and Confederate veterans had united to do him honor, the General said:

"GENTLEMEN OF THE TWO ARMIES AND NAVIES: I am very proud of the welcome you have given me. I am particularly happy to see the good will and cordiality existing between the soldiers of the two armies, and I have an enduring faith that it will always be so. I hope we shall never have a foreign war; but, if we do, I doubt not you and your children will be found fighting on the same side, and against a common enemy. I hope the day will never come when it will be necessary for us to take up arms again. I am perfectly satisfied, from travel around the world, that no foreign power desires to come in conflict with us; should any difficulty unfortunately arise, that they will always be willing to submit to friendly arbitration, and that being all that we can desire, I feel confident America has a long career of peace and prosperity before her."

General Grant prolonged his stay at San Francisco, visiting San Jose, Oakland, Belmont, Stockton, and other attractive places in the vicinity, until October 9th, when he embarked on the steamer "St. Paul" for Oregon, the harbor shipping dipping their colors as she passed. Arriving at Astoria on the 13th, a rousing welcome was accorded the General, who responded to the Mayor's address as follows:

"I am well pleased to again set foot in Oregon, and be received in such a kindly manner. The scenes are familiar. Every point of interest between Astoria and the Dalles returns to my memory. You have made great improvements. The hills do not look one-half so high as they did twenty-six years ago. I have never before set foot in Astoria. I have passed here eight times. There has been a great change, and I am pleased to see it. I regret that my stay will be so short, as I would be pleased to visit every portion of the North Pacific coast. It seems like returning home again. Thanking you for your kind and cordial welcome, I assure you it ever will be cherished in my memory."

At Vancouver an equally cordial greeting was extended. An address was presented to the General by Governor Ferry, to which he thus responded:

"GOVERNOR AND MEMBERS OF THE LEGISLATURE: I regret exceedingly that I shall not be able to remain long enough to visit any other portion of the Territory. I had expected to spend several weeks on the Pacific coast, but the reunion of the Army of the Tennessee, which I commanded during the late unpleasantness, was postponed for my return, and I have promised to meet them. They did not fix the day until I promised to be with them early in November; that, with other appointments, compels me to leave not later than the 17th. You can easily see the impossibility of accepting your invitation. Your statement of the producing quality of the Territory surprises and gratifies me. I lived a year on the spot on which I now stand, but never visited that portion of which you speak. I always supposed that while a part was productive that the greater share was too unproductive, except of fish and timber, to justify enough population to make a State unless there should be some mineral developments. From your statement, I have no doubt of your soon becoming a State, and we cannot have too many in this latitude."

On the 15th General Grant reached Portland, where the reception was only less magnificent than in San Francisco.

Ex-Senator Corbitt welcomed the distinguished party in a most hearty manner, and General Grant responded at some length, alluding to his early residence and acquaintance on the Pacific Coast. He concluded:

"In your remarks you have alluded to the struggles of the past. I am glad they are at an end. It never was a pleasure to me that they had a beginning. The result has left us a Nation to be proud of, strong at home, and respected abroad. Our reputation has extended beyond the civilized nations; it has penetrated even in the less civilized parts of the earth. In my travels I have noticed that foreign nations appear to respect us more than we respect ourselves. I have noticed the grandeur at which we have been estimated by other Powers, and their judgments should give us a higher estimate of our own greatness. They recognize that poverty, as they understand it, is not known with us. And the man of comparative affluence with them, is sometimes no better clad or fed than our pauper. Nowhere are there better elements of success than on the Pacific Coast. Here those who fought on opposite sides during the War are now peacefully associated together in a country of which they all have the same right to be proud. I thank the people again for this reception."

At Salem, Oregon City, Aurora, Evans, and other stopping-places, the ovation was spontaneous and hearty, the whole population turning out to honor him. The General was delighted with his Oregon trip, and returned to San Francisco October 20th. There was more banqueting, more receptions and civilities; and after a hurried trip to the Yo Semite Valley and Sacramento, he bade a final adieu to San Francisco, and on the 25th of October started Eastward. On the way he visited some of the most important points, especially the mining regions of Nevada, in which he took a good deal of interest. He spent several days at Virginia City, where he made a neat little speech to the miners, saying that nothing he received abroad gave him such pleasure as the reception here. True, his greeting was honest and hearty, but it showed merely the esteem felt for our country by foreign nations. "It would have been quite different," he added, "a century ago. Now we are regarded as the most powerful nation on earth. We have much which European nations have not. We have a population which as yet does not threaten to crowd any inhabited district or exhaust the productiveness of the soil. We have an extensive soil and immense undeveloped resources to exhaust before our population will become so dense as to make the raising of sufficient to live on the problem. In this respect we have great promise for the future. The fact of the matter is, we are more thought of abroad than we think of ourselves. Yet, at the same time, we think considerable of ourselves, and we, in fact, are a little conceited over our advantage. [Laughter.] Newspapers and politicians, however, think there are a good many bad people in the world, and that things are on the verge of ruin, but I guess we are all right. [Laughter.] Still we can be improved. If I was not an American I would not dare talk this for fear of being mobbed. [Laughter.] I thank you all for this kindly expression of your esteem."

The journey Eastward was made in a leisurely manner, the people everywhere along the route greeting him with the utmost enthusiasm; and on the 5th of November his two and a half years' wanderings were over, and he found himself really "home again" among his old friends and neighbors at Galena.

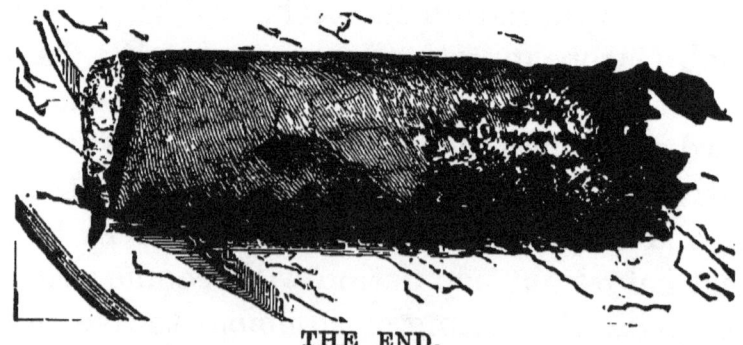

THE END.
An old Veteran left by General Grant in San Francisco.

www.ingramcontent.com/pod-product-compliance
Lightning Source LLC
Chambersburg PA
CBHW022024240426
43667CB00042B/1115